Crypto Profit

Your expert guide to financial freedom through cryptocurrency investing

by Peter Bryant, 'The Crypto Prof.'

www.thecryptoprof.com

DEDICATION

To Freya, for your enduring belief,
patience and support.

Crypto Profit

Your expert guide to financial freedom through cryptocurrency investing.

by Peter Bryant (as told to Ian Rowland)

First edition

Welcome to Crypto Profit!

This book is supplied principally from my website:

www.thecryptoprof.com

The world of crypto changes so fast, and is such a huge topic, that to cover it comprehensively in a single book is impossible. This is why I provide many additional resources on the website, including background data, supplementary material and regular updates (also available by email).

You will see references to this website content throughout this book. You don't *need* this additional content to read this book or to use the information in it. However, you will probably find it useful.

So let's get started and learn how to make crypto profit!

Have fun!

— Peter Bryant

BMus (Hons.), MSc (Lond.), ADHP (NC). UKCP

Contents

I'm Obviously Wrong... Right?

In theory, you could reduce this book to a single sentence:

You are not taking cryptocurrency investing as seriously as you should.

It is very likely that you think I'm wrong. Based on everything you've heard, read in the papers, seen online and been told by friends or even investment experts, you probably think I'm mad or dangerously deluded. Perhaps you think my next book will be on perpetual motion machines or that I'll try to sell you shares in London Bridge.

This is *precisely* why I've written this book. If nearly everyone agreed with me, I could have saved myself the trouble.

I have spoken to thousands of investors about the ideas I present in these pages. Almost every time, I've met the same knee-jerk reaction: a lengthy explanation as to why I'm wrong and why anyone investing in these currencies is a fool who will lose their capital (& deserve to).

At a recent networking event, I happened to mention that I believe cryptocurrencies are a viable investment. Before I could add any of my reasons, I was called an idiot to my face by another (traditional) investment manager. It transpired that he was not aware that the price of bitcoin had, over the past decade, risen more quickly *than any other investment in history*.

The fact that this investment manager knew nothing about bitcoin was sadly predictable. At the time, the volatility of cryptocurrencies had helped me, in my first 12 months of trading, to produce an average of 21% net profitability across all my client accounts (representing over $10 million of trading capital). My Sharpe ratio (a technical indication of risk/reward potential) stood at 2.1:1. For comparison, an investment in the S&P500 over the past 25 years has yielded a Sharpe ratio of 1:1 with an average return of 6.67%.

In plain English: I was being called an idiot for producing over three times the annual stock market return (over a very positive year) with less risk than holding that investment for 25 years in the S&P500.

If all this confuses you — and don't worry, it should — then this book is for you.

After reading this book, I hope you will want to trade and invest in cryptocurrencies. I will show you how to achieve significant profits by investing at the right time with the right strategies. I will also give you tools and resources — identified by a [T] symbol — to help you invest sensibly, with minimal risk but maximum reward potential.

My main concern is not that you might disagree with me. My main concern is that you might agree with me yet still not invest in cryptocurrencies.

If you disagree with me, great! Please let me know why via my website (www.thecryptoprof.com). Disagreement is excellent as it leads to learning, connection and correction. The worst option is to passively agree with what I say then put this book to one side while countless fantastic opportunities for crypto profit pass you by.

Today's cryptocurrency market represents a highly asymmetric environment — a low risk, high return opportunity unlike any other investment vehicle in history. This won't be the case forever so it is important to capitalise on this opportunity *now*. Coincidentally, the traditional economic and geo-political climate is at or near its peak level of risk. By the time you finish this book, I hope you will see how it can help you, over the next decade, to achieve greater financial freedom than you would ever have thought possible. I'll say it once more:

You are not taking cryptocurrency investing as seriously as you should.

Think I'm wrong? Good. Let me tell you why I think I'm right. Welcome to Crypto Profit.

Peter Bryant

– Winchester, UK.

2020

The Million Dollar Pizza

Here's an historic event involving pizza.

On May 18th, 2010, a man called Laszlo based in Florida wanted some pizza. Although he could have just ordered it from a nearby pizza place, he figured he'd try a new idea. Laszlo belonged to a website, bitcointalk.org, devoted to an entirely new type of digital currency called bitcoin. He made an offer: if anyone would order his pizza for him, Laszlo offered to send them 10,000 bitcoin.

Jercos, in London, saw the offer four days later. Using his credit card, he phoned Laszlo's local pizza joint and arranged for $25 worth of pizza to be delivered to Laszlo. Once the pizza had arrived, Laszlo kept his half of the deal and paid Jercos the promised 10,000 bitcoin. This was the first time in history that bitcoin was used to purchase tangible (and apparently very tasty) goods. The 10,000 bitcoin that Jercos now owned subsequently increased slightly in value: to $200 *million*. Yes, you read that right:

Cost: $25.

Subsequent value: $200 million.

This isn't just a story about an historic event. It's also my favourite introduction to the notion of *opportunity cost*, which means exactly what the name suggests: the cost of *not* taking advantage of an opportunity. You can miss an opportunity in two ways: by not knowing about it or by taking actions that *exclude* you from the opportunity. In this instance, Laszlo suffered a significant cost (giving up bitcoin subsequently worth $200 million) to provide the opportunity for someone else to obtain those same bitcoin for $25.

As you may have noticed from the story, four days elapsed between Laszlo making his offer and Jercos acting on it. During this time, anyone who saw the offer could have responded and made themselves 10,000 bitcoin better off... but they didn't. Why not? Did they not believe that the offer was lucrative, or at least *potentially* so? This seems to have been the case, since Laszlo had to prompt the community for a response on May 21st, saying, "So nobody wants to buy me pizza? Is the bitcoin amount too low?"

Of course, someone would have had to be extremely prescient, not to say optimistic, to value the opportunity at $200 million. However, anyone in 2010 with an account at bitcointalk.org knew the value of bitcoin was likely to increase, given that it was the first globally available autonomous digital currency. They just didn't know *when* it would become more valuable and by *how much*.

If you had quizzed anyone in 2010 and asked them how much a single bitcoin would be worth in 2017, very few would have guessed $20,000. Those who did predict anything like this sort of value were routinely mocked by most pundits. Yet they turned out to be right.

In the early 2010s almost everyone believed bitcoin to be a fad. Anyone who owned bitcoin saw it as more of a passing interest or technological hobby than a legitimate investment that would, over the next few years, significantly outperform *every other investment in history*.

People underestimated bitcoin then and most investors still do today. The critics of bitcoin and other cryptocurrencies fail to see the true value of cryptocurrencies in the context of the broader economy. If you want to take a cynical view, it's easy to suggest that a digital currency is risky if it doesn't appear to be used anywhere and its value can fluctuate by thousands of dollars a day based on public speculation. However, bitcoin started to make people extremely wealthy, and outperform every other type of investment, as early as 2013. Since then, the entire cryptocurrency sector (with bitcoin leading the charge) has demonstrated remarkable growth in genuine usage, technological development and global adoption.

Little by little, people are beginning to understand the extraordinary potential of cryptocurrencies and the remarkable technology behind them. What's more, we have long since passed the stage where cryptocurrencies can be dismissed as 'having nothing to do with the real world'. As we move through the 2020s, the chances are higher than ever that your payments for groceries or online goods routinely pass through a cryptocurrency network. Global financial institutions such as Santander and American Express have already adopted cryptocurrency technology. Why? Because it offers greater security and simplicity, yet lower fees, than their current systems. Later in this book, I'll explain more about these remarkable practical benefits and how they are achieved.

The effects of the mass adoption of cryptocurrencies have not yet trickled down to common public knowledge. Today, only a number of 'early adopter' large corporate entities are realising the many benefits of crypto. It is only a matter of time before these benefits become obvious to everyone and cryptocurrencies become widely adopted, replacing more traditional ways to exchange value.

Investors should be aware that the next increase in the value of bitcoin and other cryptos will be the biggest yet. It will involve an exponentially larger amount of capital, from a substantially larger number of users, than the last large movement in 2017 when the value of a single bitcoin hit $20,000. Missing out on this profit opportunity still haunts some investors I know who witnessed the very first stages of cryptocurrency development in 2012. They could have purchased as many bitcoin as they wanted when the price was $0.10. In 2015, one of my current clients purchased two hundred ether (another cryptocurrency) for £50 and watched its value rise to over £200,000 in two years.

Why, in a book about investing, have I taken the time to tell you a story about pizza? Because it's a good introduction to a simple, but important, subject. As I will show in this book, the current financial system that we all know and find reassuringly familiar is broken, or at least breaking. It's based on 'fiat' currency (money backed by nothing but trust) and a dizzying spiral of debt that is simply unsustainable in the long-term. Sooner or later, something's got to give. Cryptocurrencies provide brilliant and practical solutions to these problems. They have moved on from being an interesting technological idea to being a practical way to exchange value in a fast, secure way that no fiat currencies can match.

Imagine you could go back in time and invest in the development of national electricity networks in the 1890s or the internet in the 1990s. Happily armed with the knowledge of how these technologies would thrive and prosper, and become practically indispensable, you'd be able to make quite a profit, wouldn't you?

It's the same today with cryptocurrencies. Over the next decade, digital currencies and the technology that powers them will revolutionise almost every aspect of our economies, financial systems and industries. Currently, the financial world is suffering from a bad case of information overload, insecure systems and errors with intermediaries charging exorbitant fees that we have no choice but to accept. The new world, made possible by cryptocurrency technology, will be one of smart data, 100% secure transactions and contracts with no errors, no intermediaries and very small fees. It will be a world running more efficiently, effectively and economically than ever before.

I will show you how to harness (and, indirectly, contribute to) this growth by investing in cryptocurrencies with the strongest fundamental support and greatest profit potential.

My primary focus is not short-term gains measured over a few days (although short-term profits do play a part) but on long-term growth of the cryptocurrency market.

First, lets really understand why cryptocurrencies and the technology that powers them is so desperately needed.

Profit Points

- Cryptocurrencies are a unique asset class that most investors believe is, at best, perplexing and intimidating and, at worst, terrifying and foolhardy.

- Any cryptocurrency investor needs to change the way they think about their exponential investment in crypto, in contrast to other (linear) investments they may hold such as shares (see the section on page 87).

- Valuing any cryptocurrency investment opportunity requires you to distance yourself psychologically from the current price. Focus instead on where the price has been (long and short-term) and where it may go, based on fundamentals (which I'll discuss in the next chapter). This helps you to get a better idea as to the true value of the cryptocurrency. At the time of writing, every cryptocurrency referenced within this book is severely below its true long-term value, which represents a set of fantastic investment opportunities.

- Don't be afraid to buy in small amounts of capital if the price is already low in order to avoid a severe opportunity cost. The definition of 'low' will change with the market conditions and fundamentals. It is generally a good rule of thumb to consider 'low' as below half of the most recent yearly high.

- Don't be fooled when prices seem boring or do not appear to be moving. When things get exciting, it is usually too late to make the best returns.

- If you feel like you have missed the crypto boat, don't worry. You haven't. 2017 was merely a wake–up call.

- There can be an element of self-fulfilling prophecy with *any* set of investments — including cryptocurrencies. When the majority of investors favour investment, the price goes up thereby (apparently) justifying the investment and spurring further confidence. This creates an opportunity for investors to increase their portfolios by using the smaller movements to take advantage of the larger movements. Trading in this way can give you compound results in an exponential asset class which can be extremely profitable.

[T] Use the CryptoProf Valuation Tool to help you evaluate your cryptocurrency investments in terms of risk and reward. You can find this on the cryptoprof website under the 'Tools' menu.

A Broken System (And How To Fix It)

In this book, I'll express my confidence about three things:

* Cryptocurrencies are here to stay.

* They will enjoy greater acceptance and more widespread adoption as time goes by.

* They represent a brilliant once-in-a-lifetime investment opportunity.

Cryptocurrencies will thrive because they are *useful*. More specifically, they are the *only* way to solve some really *big* problems.

One of these big problems is that the global financial system we all know is broken, unsustainable, expensive and bound to fail. In fact, it's really *three* big problems in one. Let's look at the problems first, then see why cryptocurrencies, and the ingenious technology behind them, provide a brilliant solution.

Problem 1: Fatally Flawed Fiat Currencies

Imagine you are the director of a company, founded in 1694, that is still trading today. Your company was the first of its kind to gain a royal warrant. You have a strong reputation and exert considerable power within your home market and, to a certain extent, the world. When the company was first formed, one thousand shares were distributed to shareholders. Your firm has a policy of releasing one thousand shares every year to new investors, with the original shareholders diluting their stake by between 2% and 3%. Would you consider this to be a good investment?

This hypothetical company is called the Bank of England and its 'product' is the Great British Pound (GBP). The value of money, like any other commodity, product or service, is determined by supply and demand. If you increase the supply of a product, assuming constant demand, its price will go down in proportion to the additional supply. Conversely, if you restrict supply then the price generally goes up.

You might think it works slightly differently with currencies, since a pound coin is still a pound coin even if you create more of them. This is true if you look at the currency *in isolation*. However, as we all know, money by itself is useless. You can't eat it, drink it, drive it, watch it or have any fun with it. Money only becomes useful, and has any meaning, when you exchange it for goods and services. This is referred to as the currency's purchasing power.

The only way to determine the purchasing power of a currency is to assess, over a given period of time, what you can exchange it for in terms of everyday purchases (such as bread and milk) or the purchasing power of some other currency (for example, whether a pound buys you more bread than a dollar).

There was a time when currencies were backed by physical commodities such as gold or silver. To some extent, this protected and preserved the currency's purchasing power even if a central bank created more of it. At one time, if the Bank of England decided to print more £1 notes, it made sure that each of them was backed by an asset that was enjoying a corresponding rise in value. For example, if you look at gold you will see that, neglecting short-term volatility, it has been rising in value for its entire history.

However, today's currencies are what are called 'fiat' currencies (from the Latin for 'let it be done'). A fiat currency isn't backed by anything except a government or central bank *decreeing* that its notes and tokens have some value. Another way of looking at it is to say a fiat currency only has value so long as enough people *believe* it has value and purchasing power.

If you buy a used car from me, I'll accept some pounds (or dollars or whatever) because I *trust* that tomorrow I'll be able to use them to buy life's essentials, such as bread, milk and fine, vintage wine. When I want to buy something, I hope the seller will accept my money on the same basis: not because it's backed by gold or any other valuable substance (which it isn't) but because they *believe* the money I hand over has purchasing power today and will still have some next week.

There's a big problem with all this: gold can't evaporate into thin air but belief can. So can purchasing power. This isn't just a theoretical possibility confined to dusty economics textbooks. It's what happens in real life. What's more, it doesn't happen by accident. Rather more alarmingly, it's what happens *by design*.

Let's get back to the story of the Bank of England. As we've seen, if you increase the supply of a currency its purchasing power decreases. When the pound was backed by solid, shiny gold bars, this effect was minimised because gold reliably increased in value over time and this stabilised the currency to some extent.

However, on September 19th, 1931, the Bank decided to take the pound 'off the gold standard'. It was no longer backed by anything except the Bank's *decree* that it had value and the collective belief of the people using the currency. From that time onwards, on each of the Bank's tokens (pound notes), it merely promised to pay the bearer the sum of 'one pound'. Not one pound of gold or silver or anything else. Just 'a pound'. In other words, 'this piece of paper is worth one of these pieces of paper'. This rather circular promise was written on every pound note until the £1 coin took over in 1983.

Adopting a fiat currency creates new possibilities but also new problems. One of the possibilities is that a bank can print as much money as it wants (because it doesn't have to have any gold to back up the value of each note or coin). It's possible to see this as a good thing, if you take a very narrow and short-term view. For example, it means a bank can print money to lend to lots of start-up businesses or to invest in big corporations, thereby stimulating the economy. The big problem is that the bank might get carried away with the idea of printing money and end up seriously in debt. In fact, it could reach the point where it has no realistic chance of ever paying off its debt.

You might think the Bank of England would never do something so wanton and reckless. After all, aren't banks run by serious, sober financial experts, noble custodians of capital, who want to make sure the economy is always on a sound footing?

Unfortunately, this is not the case. In March 2019, the Bank of England reported that it is in £1.8 trillion in debt while the United Kingdom's Gross Domestic Product (GDP) is about £2.62 trillion. Therefore, if the Bank of England wanted to pay off its debt in one go, it would need to use 86% of the country's 'annual turnover' (not profit) to do so.

If the Bank of England ran into difficulties, you might suppose an even bigger bank could come to its rescue and 'bail it out' if necessary. Again, this is unfortunately not the case. The most likely contender would be the American Federal Reserve, but it's a case of 'bigger bank, bigger problem'. In 1971 it stopped aligning the dollar with physical assets so, it too was just a fiat currency. Furthermore, it is in significantly greater debt than the Bank of England. It currently has $23 trillion of debt against a GDP of $19.36 trillion. It would need to use 116% of its annual turnover to eradicate the problem completely. This is not going to happen. Costs are escalating and paying back even a small amount of the national debt is extremely challenging.

In fact, the Fed's debt has risen by over 10% in two years to its highest level ever. What's more, the global default rate on debt at an international scale — called negative yielding debt — has been increasing at its fastest rate ever, reaching over $16 trillion across the entire world and jumping by $10 trillion in 2019. (For a sobering visualisation of this fact, visit the clock resource on the cryptoprof website.)

Is there any sign of things getting better? Quite the contrary. These central banks are seeing their debts grow at an alarming rate due to compound interest charges of around 4% in the case of the UK and 8.7% in the USA. The interest alone accounts for an additional debt of over £50 billion in the UK and over $500 billion in the USA, this minimises the effect of the payments attempting to reduce the problem. Essentially, both the UK and the USA are on the verge of bankruptcy. The same pattern is found all over the globe. Across the world, countries are in debt to each other by an unprecedented $250 trillion. This means that every man, woman & child throughout the world effectively owes $33,000 to someone else. What is even worse, is that due to compound interest, the debt is growing by the day.

This is a dire situation and one that is clearly unsustainable. However, it's even worse than it seems to be. You see, you could be forgiven for thinking that this shaky, teetering tower of debt is the result of something having gone horribly wrong with the global financial system. Maybe there is time to put things right and steer the car back onto the road? Maybe we can revive this patient? Unfortunately, no. This situation is not the result of rotten luck or a few fixable mistakes. *It's the known, predictable outcome of deliberate and intentional policy.* In other words, we can't hope for things to be put right because, as far as the central banks and their policies are concerned, nothing has gone wrong. There's nothing to fix. The car is heading off into the ditch and towards the tree because that's where the banks steered it. They were following a map called 'quantitative easing'.

Let's take a closer look at this. Since 1971, many countries with large economies, including the UK, USA and China, have been printing and circulating more of their currency as a way to stimulate their economies. This policy, elegantly entitled 'quantitative easing', can be seen as a good move *in the short-term.* Businesses boom, property prices increase, and everyone invests in bonds, businesses and the stock market. Prices inflate rapidly and reliably resulting in the overall growth of the country and its economy, if looked at in purely statistical terms.

However, there is a problem with all this growth. In order to pay for it, a country has two options. One is to secure additional capital (from an international bank or another country) and therefore acquire more debt. The other is to create more money simply by printing it. Both options weaken the country's currency by decreasing its purchasing power in proportion to the amount of new currency created. This decrease in purchasing power is called inflation. The consensus among world banks is that a 'healthy' level of annual inflation is between 2% and 3%. This means that if you have a £50 bank note in your pocket, it should ideally lose £1 of its value (in terms of its original purchasing power) over 1 year. Over 10 years, your £50 is worth £38.15. Over 50 years, for example if it's held in a cash pension, it's worth just £2.93. (You can use the inflation calculator tool on the cryptoprof website to understand this further.)

This steady erosion of value might seem quite alarming, but the picture is even worse than it seems. This slow, steady loss of purchasing power is what happens when inflation is kept within what are deemed to be 'healthy' limits. Not all countries manage this. In 2019, there were 16 countries with an inflation rate above 10%. Imagine *everything* you might want to buy being 10% more expensive now than it was a year ago! Once inflation gets out of control, there's really no limit to how bad the situation can get. On the 19th of April 2019, the level of inflation in Venezuela was recorded at 282,972%. (As a side note, it is no coincidence that bitcoin is used more extensively in Venezuela than almost anywhere else. The Venezuelan people have discovered that it is far less volatile, and more likely to maintain its value, than their fiat currency. I believe it won't be long before other people, in other countries, reach similar conclusions.)

Not all countries are in the same dire straits as Venezuela. However, *all* fiat currencies are, by their very design, getting weaker and weaker in terms of their purchasing power. When the pound (the oldest currency in existence) was first minted, one pound was worth twelve troy ounces of silver. The currency was known as 'pounds sterling' because 'sterling' refers to a specific grade of silver (92.5% pure). The pound's original purchasing power was equivalent to about £200 today. Putting it another way, due to inflation, a pound today has less than 0.05% of its original purchasing power.

History provides many examples of what happens when the oversupply of a fiat currency is taken to extremes: hyperinflation. Hyperinflation means the government's control of currency and its value is so weak that its purchasing power plummets, so even a single loaf of bread costs 10,000,000 units of the currency. Hyperinflation has occurred many times in history, including several instances during the 20th century (Germany, Zimbabwe and Hungary being notable examples).

The fact is, hyperinflation could happen in any economy at any time, given an extended period of quantitative easing. In fact, hyperinflation is essentially *inevitable* for any currency that is not backed by a physical commodity (such as gold) and has been subject to quantitative easing (printing more money) for a significant period.

Is there a way to stop hyperinflation? Yes. By paying off its debt, a government can regain control over its currency. It can do this in several ways:

1. Sell assets that it owns.

2. Raise taxes such as income tax, corporation tax or sales taxes (such as VAT).

3. Print more money (quantitative easing) and reduce interest rates to stimulate personal and corporate borrowing.

For the most part, over the past fifty years, mainstream economies have preferred the third option. This *can* be a viable strategy. However, it should only be used as a last resort and, even then, only on a temporary, short-term basis. Unfortunately, major economies have been pursuing this policy for decades. You don't have to be an economics genius to see where this leads. Taking a couple of aspirin one evening can ease a headache. Taking a hundred every day for a week does not lead to anywhere good.

Since 2007, the USA has created $4.5 trillion out of thin air by selling bonds to investors that are effectively worthless if the underlying currency collapses. This creation of capital occurred during three distinct periods (2008-9, 2010-12 and 2013-14). Donald Trump is keen to start a fourth wave of quantitative easing, having spent an additional $1 trillion a year since he came to office in 2016.

The US national debt now stands at $23 trillion and rising. The interest payments alone were $325 billion in 2018 and are forecast to rise to $762 billion by 2026. At this rate, by 2021 the US will pay more in interest than it does to fund its military (which is the most expensive in the world). The UK is not much better, having printed £430 billion over the same time period.

This story of the switch to fiat currencies and the many associated problems was always destined to end badly. However, it was made a lot worse by the rise of the dollar as the world's first global currency. Let's take a moment to see why.

The Driver And The Ditch

The United States dollar (USD) is the most successful currency in history. Every country in the world trades in USD despite the US only representing 6% of the world's land mass. How did the US dollar become so ubiquitous and powerful and why should this be considered a problem?

The story starts with gold. By the early part of the 20th century, the USA had amassed extensive reserves of gold. These reserves were so vast that during World War Two, America was able to finance its war effort by using its gold reserves as collateral for short-term loan arrangements with its allies.

Because the largest amount of gold was found in America at the time, gold was naturally traded in dollars. After the war, the market for dollars increased dramatically as countries started to pay back their debt using the dollar rather than their own national currencies. America wasn't interested in receiving francs for its gold — it wanted to be paid in the dollar.

This was codified in the Bretton-Woods agreement of 1944. Because the US dollar was so powerful, every currency in the world was pegged to it rather than to gold. The idea was that since the dollar was backed by gold, every currency was, by extension, backed by gold to some degree. For the first time in history, every currency on Earth, apart from the US dollar, had no tangible asset backing it.

Backed by the ever-increasing price of gold (a finite global commodity, much like a cryptocurrency — the difference being that the total amount of gold in the world is unknown), the US dollar got stronger during the 1950s and 60s. The US was unable to completely corner the gold market as it was already a global commodity. Some African countries were annually mining twenty times as much gold as the US by 1970. However, a new commodity was growing in demand on an international scale much more quickly than gold: oil.

During the 19th and 20th centuries, the USA was both the world's largest producer *and* consumer of oil. America developed significant influence over the world's oil market earlier than any other country. The world's first oil well was developed in Pennsylvania in 1859 and oil has been a large part of the US economy ever since.

At that time, the USA controlled so much of the oil market that, between 1960 and 1965, fourteen Middle Eastern countries organised themselves into what became OPEC (the Organization of Petroleum Exporting Countries). This deliberately excluded the USA.

Oil helped to literally fuel worldwide technological developments like global transport (cars, aeroplanes and ships), the rapid development of infrastructure (such as road construction and heating) and even food, clothes, toys and entertainment media (plastic goods and plastic packaging). It could be said that throughout the industrialised world, modern societies essentially depended (and as is becoming increasingly obvious and problematic, still do depend) upon the consumption of oil.

Hence the dollar became the default currency for two of the most important global commodities. Just as English is the default language of the internet, the US dollar became the default currency for trade. Today, the US dollar is the reserve currency for almost every country on earth. It accounts for over 60% of global bank reserves and 40% of global debt.

This huge degree of consolidation around one currency would be risky and problematic under any circumstances. However, it's *especially* problematic for one good reason we've already looked at: *the dollar has no intrinsic value*. It is no longer backed by gold or anything else, so it only has value because the people who use it *believe* it has. Furthermore, it has been devaluing by around 3.24% every year, or around 2000% since it was first introduced.

When the purchasing power of the dollar becomes sufficiently weak, which is more a case of 'when' than 'if', it will hyperinflate and its perceived value will drop to zero. When this happens, the US economy will collapse, and the effects will be much worse than the fallout from the 2008 financial crisis (provided there are no contingency plans). It's a mistake for everyone to get on the same bus if the driver's heading for the ditch.

It's easy to draw conclusions from all this. Today's prevailing financial system, based on fiat currencies, is unsustainable. It is completely baseless and predicated on the systematic devaluation of currencies over time to the point where one of two things can happen. Either the currency gets devalued or it gets replaced by something else, such as a completely new currency (for example, the Euro, introduced across Europe in 1999 which had replaced fifteen fiat currencies by 2008).

The global banking system does not present a very healthy or promising picture: spiralling debt that can never be paid off, untamed inflation and currencies built on nothing but belief that are destined to lose their purchasing power *by design*.

You might think it couldn't get any worse, but you would be wrong. I said the global financial system is broken and that there are really three problems in one. The first was the inherent flaws of fiat currencies. Now let's look at the second problem. It's a pretty scary one called fractional reserve banking.

Problem 2: Fractured Fractional Reserves

From the outside, the modern banking system can appear quite robust. You deposit your money in the bank of your choice and they look after it for you. Their large, imposing buildings and familiar branding inspire a sense of trust and confidence. Unfortunately, when you look behind the curtain, the wizard doesn't seem quite so powerful.

When you make a deposit at a bank, the money changes legal ownership and becomes one of the bank's assets. In fact, the bank refers to your capital as Assets Under Management (AUM). The bank can lend this money to a borrower (in return for a nice fee). Of course, you have no say over who they choose to lend it to and you might, just possibly, disapprove of some of their choices.

JP Morgan invested in companies that helped to ship $1.3 billion of illegal cocaine around the world. HSBC assisted Mexican crime cartels to launder $881 million over five years. When HSBC's involvement came to light, they paid a $1.9 billion fine but not one of their employees lost their job. Strangely enough, neither of these banks tends to feature these episodes in their advertising. For links to these news stories (and more) see the 'Bank' tab on the website.

Let's continue to look at the murky world of fractional reserve banking. You deposit some money with your bank and they loan it to whoever they want. Banks and financial institutions have a system for assessing which people and businesses they consider a good risk. This is called a credit score. Customers who banks believe will repay their debt on time and with the correct fees (based on past behaviour) have a high credit score and everyone else has a low one.

The implicit assumption is that someone with a history of repaying their debts will continue to do so. Unfortunately, as we saw with the 2008 recession, this is a far from reliable way to assess whether or not someone is credit worthy. Someone with an impeccable track record can suddenly become unable to repay their debts. This can happen for several reasons such as difficult economic circumstances causing a customer with a high credit score to lose their job. If this happens to enough people, the creditor will be in serious trouble. The system is extremely fragile and when things go wrong, they go *catastrophically* wrong.

However, let's say it is generally the case that people pay their debts and the system functions reasonably well. The bank is able to return your money when you ask for it, such as when you go to withdraw some cash or when you buy something with your debit card.

In an ideal world, the borrower (with a high credit score) returns the money loaned by the bank plus fees and interest. The bank keeps the fees and interest so its employees get their salary. Everyone is happy. You have a safe, convenient place to keep your money and you can withdraw it whenever you want (which, if the loan hasn't yet been repaid comes from the capital deposits of other customers). The borrower can get a loan and the bank makes a profit.

There are some rather strange aspects to this scenario. For example, you are the only one taking any risk (when you deposit your money) yet you get very little return. By being one of the bank's customers, you implicitly front the capital for the loan. However, you receive little or no interest because the bank keeps it all. The bank is playing roulette with your money, but if it wins, it keeps the profits.

The system may be a little unfair in terms of risk and reward, but at least your money is safe and secure, right? Alas, not so. The supposed 'safety' is an illusion. Let me explain why.

In the 17th century, banks were routinely running into liquidity issues caused by withdrawals temporarily outweighing deposits. To solve this problem, the banks came up with an ingenious ruse. They invented the concept of *fractional reserve* banking, which is a beautifully elegant way of saying 'lending more money than they really have'. The idea was that commercial banks could lend more money than they held on deposit in order to cover their customer withdrawals on a temporary basis. Whenever they did so, they incurred a debt from their country's central bank. This practice seems safe enough if you *assume* that a bank, being such an important part of society and playing a role in the life of every person and every company, will never go out of business.

When it was introduced, fractional reserve banking allowed banks to lend up to *nine* times whatever they held in terms of assets. This meant that if you deposited £100 with a bank, they could lend £900 against your deposit (which acted as the security) to anyone they felt was likely to pay them back.

Over time, regulations became less strict and banks started exceeding this nine-to-one ratio of loans to deposits. Today, most banks maintain capital reserves of just 10% of their balance sheets or even less. As a result, when things *do* go wrong the problems are magnified by a factor of ten. This is what happened during the 2008 financial crisis, when previously very creditworthy people stopped paying their debts as they had no jobs and, therefore, no money.

This is one reason why banks and financial institutions impose limits on withdrawals. You may have noticed that banks today don't allow electronic payments above a set threshold. This is partly to combat fraud but it also helps keep the bank solvent, since it prevents too many people trying to withdraw their money too quickly.

A bank's desire to stay solvent can sometimes get rather desperate. In 2019, the third largest bank in Denmark, Jyske Bank, was offering a *negative* 0.5% mortgage. In other words, you would pay back *less* than they loaned to you. The bank was happy to take a small loss to attract enough capital to stay solvent. (If you think I am making this up, see the 'Mortgage' tab on the website.)

Fractional reserve banking has become the global standard almost by necessity. Banks need a certain level of liquidity to operate and so need to be able to lend more money than they hold in deposits. This gives rise to an obvious problem: if too many of a bank's customers all choose to withdraw their money at the same time, the bank can't possibly pay them all and the system collapses. This is not just an alarming but theoretical possibility. It actually happens.

In 2007, the fourth largest bank in the UK, called Northern Rock, celebrated its 170th year in business. Then, in May of that year, everything changed. The bank's mortgage department had taken on too much risk and suffered heavy losses when the sub-prime mortgage crisis hit America. As a result, Northern Rock asked the Bank of England for emergency funds. This caused a wave of panic among Northern Rock customers who withdrew £2 billion over the course of a few days (around 10% of the bank's deposits). The bank struggled to pay them all, which only prompted more panic and more withdrawals. Outside every branch, long lines formed of people waiting to withdraw their money. Eventually, the UK government had to step in, bail out Northern Rock with £37 billion of taxpayer's money and nationalise the bank.

As we have seen, the value of all fiat currencies depreciates by an average of 2% per year even during periods of so-called prosperity. During times of economic stress, they can depreciate by thousands of percent very quickly. The UK government, like every other major government, cannot feasibly reduce the amount of borrowed capital significantly enough to lower the level of inflation. For one thing, population growth means there is an ever-increasing number of people who want to use a currency.

What's more, it has become standard procedure for banks to leverage a currency nine times over just to stay solvent. This 'leveraged' capital is just a number on a bank's balance sheet backed by nothing more than a promise to settle later. This is fine unless many people all want their money at the same time, at which point the bank collapses. This has happened several times and there's no reason to think it won't happen again.

So far, we've looked at two big problems of the financial systems we all rely on every day. The first was the rise and inevitable failure of fiat currencies, or money based on nothing but belief. The second was the 'ticking time bomb' of fractional reserve banking, or banks pretending they have nine or ten times more money than they really do. The third problem is the one you can hear rumbling in the background: the slow, clanking, clapped out machinery of a wheezing, inefficient system that's on the verge of collapse.

Problem #3: Fat Fees And Leaky Pipes

It's bad news when a system is expensive (even if it works well). It's also bad news when a system is inefficient and unfit for its purpose (even if it's cheap). The current global financial system manages to offer the worst of both worlds: it's expensive *and* inefficient.

Once upon a time, there was no need for banks (or their fees). Until the invention of modern banking in the 17th century, transactions either took place instantaneously, with both parties receiving their side of the deal at the same time or were recorded via a manual ledger. For a transaction to take place, each party (or their representative) had to be physically present. There was usually a physical medium of exchange and the transaction was either settled immediately or very soon after the exchange was agreed.

When people started using tokens and pieces of paper to represent value, transactions could occur over a greater geographical area (for example by post) without both parties being present at the same time. This gave rise to the need for someone to act as an intermediary. After all, I could *claim* that I've sent you $100 but without a third party regulating the transaction you have no way to check if this is true.

A more sophisticated ledger system — regulated by an independent party — was needed to keep track of debits and credits during transactions that might take days or even weeks to complete. The embryonic banking industry created the systems and processes that enabled transactions to take place over any distance or period, with both parties feeling they could trust the bank to be fair, neutral and accurate.

Banks were quick to position themselves as the 'honest broker' that the rest of us could rely on, and to create the impression that they were safe, secure palaces of financial rectitude. They realised that this was the key to immense profits.

To validate transactions, banks and financial institutions charge a commission (typically 1% to 2%, but it can be as high as 5%). This system is so profitable that banks can provide an almost free service to personal users in the hope that they will buy other products (such as a mortgage). Personal bank accounts are a highly profitable loss leader for the banking sector. A 2014 study calculated that the average American pays $279,002 in interest in their lifetime, amounting to trillions of dollars every single year. What often seems to be 'free banking' is almost always nothing of the sort. (For more information, see the 'Interest' tab on the website.)

Over time, as the global banking sector has been required to complete more and more tasks, these fees have become larger and more widespread. This is excellent for banks, regulators, financial organisations and payment processors. It's not so great for end users such as businesses and retail customers. The global banking sector costs consumers around $1.6 trillion per year — a figure that has only ever increased, year on year, since modern banking began. This figure includes charges for processing cash and administrating bank accounts, merchant services fees, money transfer fees and foreign exchange fees.

I freely admit that this system worked well up to a point. Had it not done so, we wouldn't have seen the rise of the banking industry as we know it. However, it's not just an expensive system, with the banks charging a fee for practically every transaction, but also an extraordinarily inefficient and insecure one.

As banking and transactions have become more complex, the system has become extremely cumbersome and dilapidated. Today, if you wish to send money using a bank, your funds will be transferred through an average of *seven* different institutions before reaching the recipient. The process involves a maze of fees, processing costs, insurance and human resources (for cash transactions, maintenance of systems and customer interaction).

All this processing is achieved through the SWIFT system (a name derived from the Society for Worldwide Interbank Financial Telecommunications). This system, used by most of the banks in the world, was invented in 1973. In other words, most of the global banking system runs on technology older than VHS tape and even more prone to errors and chewed up data.

It's true that there have been some improvements to SWIFT since its introduction. It's also true that, even today, up to 6% of all transactions fall through leaks in the pipes, so to speak, and go missing entirely. This creaking, inefficient system involves high staffing costs, expensive hardware, systems and maintenance, plus insurance on every transaction. Directly or indirectly, all these costs get passed down to you and me, the customers of the banks, who have to contend with delays, slow verification checks on every transaction and of course the fees that are built into every stage of the 'service'.

These fees can be so significant as to *impede* progress, innovation and convenience. Prior to the widespread adoption of digital money, many retailers refused debit and credit card payments despite knowing that customers spend more when using plastic than cash (see the 'Card' tab on the website for more details). Why did they refuse? Because for many merchants the fees for processing card transactions were too high to be worthwhile. Larger businesses passed these fees on to their customers in the form of an additional charge (which has recently been made illegal in some countries) or by slightly increasing their prices to absorb the cost.

Okay, so the banks cost us all a lot of money, use clunky, inefficient systems and lose 6% of all the money entrusted to their care. Nonetheless, we still need them... don't we? You may have heard it said that without banks making a lot of money, there would be nothing to fuel the economy. If you think this sounds dubious, you're right. It's true that banks have huge amounts of capital derived from fees and interest. However, they do not lend most of this to businesses and individuals. They have the capacity, via a central or government bank, to create new money out of thin air and, in the majority of cases, they choose to do this instead.

The fees that are collected from banking activities form the capital used to pay the salaries and bonuses of the bank's staff plus dividends to its shareholders. Of course, some of this money that is paid out comes back into the banking system. For example, an employee might pay part of their earnings into a pension that is ultimately owned by the bank they work for or a competitor. This, in turn, helps the banking system to achieve additional profits. This cyclical process suits the banks very well but is ultimately unsustainable.

Not-for-profit banks do exist, but they represent a tiny minority of the global banking sector. The overwhelming majority of banks are for-profit and, over the past two or three decades, have become increasingly reckless. Fuelled by the mistaken belief that they are too big to fail, they have started to take larger risks with more capital and prepared fewer contingency plans against loss.

They have also failed to prepare for 'black swan' events. A black swan event is one that is statistically very unlikely yet almost certain to happen if you have a very large data set and wait long enough. A roulette wheel coming up '12' three times in a row is freakishly unlikely, yet it is almost certain to happen at least once a week in at least one casino somewhere in the world. Black swan events can completely wipe out a bank's capital — which, of course, is actually the capital of the bank's customers or, more simply, you and me.

Far from being mere speculation, this has happened more than once. A well-known example would be the mortgage crisis of 2008 that caused the collapse of Lehman Brothers (and several other financial institutions). By definition, black swan events are unpredictable. However, whenever one occurs, various 'experts' with a talent for after-the-event prophecy can be relied on to explain that it was largely predictable all along. The financial sector may be short of many things, such as probity and a sense of caution, but it is rarely short of self-congratulatory pundits and Cassandras.

The essential frailty of the current, old-fashioned banking system was demonstrated in 2008 when the mortgage crisis, predominantly in the USA, caused $9.8 trillion to vanish from the global economy. The world's governments were able to solve the problem, to some extent, by footing the bill and, in the process, slashing interest rates effectively to zero. The banks, of course, learned many valuable lessons from this terrible catastrophe and took steps to ensure nothing like it could ever happen again. I'm joking, of course. They actually carried on exactly as before and behaved as if the disaster had never happened.

Over the next fifty years, the world will see the multi-trillion-dollar traditional banking industry shrink significantly. People will start to abandon large institutions and entrust their money elsewhere or manage it themselves. This process has already begun. Bitcoin was first mined only thirty days after the 2008 stock market crash, yet cryptocurrencies are already a multi-trillion-dollar market (based on annual trading volume). The largest exchanges (such as Binance) make billions of dollars in profit every year.

Of course, the banks want you to believe they are faithful and loyal custodians of your money who work hard to serve your interests. However, history demonstrates that this is far from the truth. Banks exploit opportunities for their own gain as far as possible and ignore or even repress anything (via lobbying) that undermines or threatens their power. This is why every bank initially vilified cryptocurrencies and denounced them with sneering scepticism bordering on hatred. They saw the threat to the monopoly they had enjoyed for centuries and, quite understandably, didn't like it at all. Hence the snarling and sneering.

These sentiments haven't softened a great deal over the past decade. All that has changed is that the banks have discovered how to use crypto technology to protect or increase their profits (largely with XRP - see page 54) and have, therefore, begun to tentatively adopt it. They still dislike the term 'cryptocurrency' so they have started using names that they think sound safer and more reassuring, such as 'blockchain' or 'on demand liquidity' (another name for XRP).

Some institutions have even created their own cryptocurrencies, such as 'JPMorgan Coin', which is ironic given that Jamie Dimon, the CEO of JP Morgan, was one of the most vocal critics of bitcoin in 2017.

The bankers like the current system because they do very well out of it. As custodians of the system they created, they can charge a fee almost every time a purchase is made, money is loaned, or a debt is incurred. The rest of us might not like the fees but we have to pay them regardless. This means we are all forced to fund the banking system that could, all too easily, collapse one morning and take our capital with it.

This concludes our survey of all that's rotten in the state of the global banking system. There is little to admire about the combination of doomed fiat currencies, the gaping flaws and mythical money of fractional reserves plus the glaring defects of a system that is expensive, inefficient and leaks like a sieve.

It is entirely realistic to suggest that all fiat currencies are in a downward spiral towards zero purchasing power and the economic system behind them is on the brink of collapse.

What would be a *better* way of doing things? How about a system that will never suffer from inflation, doesn't involve imaginary money and makes it possible to settle transactions *without* third party supervision (or fees)? How about one that enables everyone in the world to achieve the exchange of value instantly, very cheaply, with precisely zero errors or leakage?

A system like this would be pretty good, wouldn't it?

A system like this is called a cryptocurrency.

Let's look at what a cryptocurrency is and how it works.

Profit Points

- Every fiat currency is becoming dramatically weaker, in terms of purchasing power, over time. Fiat currencies are not backed by anything other than a promise to repay that cannot be kept on a long-term basis. It is likely that major currencies such as the United States Dollar (USD) and Great British Pound (GBP) will shortly hyperinflate if the economy continues to operate the way it has over the past fifty years.

- The world is in a $250 trillion debt crisis where most developed countries are almost bankrupt and paying extortionate amounts of interest to just about keep their economies working.

- Fractional reserve banking makes these issues a lot worse and will contribute to the collapse of fiat currencies (and with them, the economy as we know it) at some point in the near future.

Crypto 101: The Blockchain

As I have said, cryptocurrencies will thrive for one very simple and compelling reason: they are *useful*. They solve big problems that can't be solved any other way (as far as we know). Most importantly, they provide a new way of exchanging value that is superior to the present system in every way. To see *why* cryptocurrencies are such a revolutionary technology, let's look at how they work.

A way to transfer value digitally and instantaneously has been the 'holy grail' of computer scientists since the first two computers were connected in the 1960s. When you send an email or upload something to the internet, you are generating a copy of the file that is sent to the recipient. This works superbly well for media, documents and other forms of information and has created today's information age. Vast swathes of information have become free, open source and available to anyone who can get online.

However, the same method cannot be used to exchange value. Quite apart from the fact that it is illegal to duplicate currency, there's no way to digitise *value* and send it over the internet. Of course, you can make electronic payments via websites such as PayPal but these involve independent third-party organisations to act as processors (who take a fee for their services). These third parties also supervise the transaction to make sure it's legitimate and successful.

Is there a way for one person to transfer money to another, in such a way that both can be certain it's a fair transaction, *without* involving a third party? This certainly seems like a tough problem. How can you and I be certain that my bank balance has gone down by the precise amount that yours has gone up, and both of us are participating honestly? What if I'm dishonest and I *say* I'm transferring ten dollars to you but I secretly keep those ten dollars in my own account? For a long time, no-one had a good solution to this problem. Many experts doubted that there *was* a solution.

Cryptocurrencies provide the answer. They make it possible for anyone to achieve 100% safe, successful transfer of digitised value, so that both parties can be sure it's fair, without the need for any intermediary or regulator. They achieve this by using revolutionary technology called a blockchain.

Blockchain technology involves a constantly updated ledger that allows anyone to examine the entire history of an asset, such as bitcoin, at any time. (I am using bitcoin as my example because it was the first blockchain used for real transactions.) All bitcoin transactions are processed by the ledger, validated multiple times and stored forever in such a way that anyone can check for themselves whenever they want. Blockchain technology operates completely automatically and autonomously.

On top of this, the distributed nature of the ledger means that the transaction data is not stored on any one system or computer, but on millions of computers simultaneously. This means that cryptocurrency networks have a level of resilience even more robust than the technology that underpins websites such as Google, Facebook and Wikipedia. For a genuine bitcoin, ether or ripple transaction to malfunction, it would have to invalidate several known laws of physics. Using a blockchain via a distributed computer network is the fastest, most secure and efficient way of transacting value ever invented.

Theoretically, you can store any information on a blockchain, not just transactions and values. The data is instantly rendered indexable, searchable and, therefore, more useful. One day, hospital records, supply chain data, human resources records and many other kinds of information will be maintained, exchanged and used via blockchain technology.

Blockchain Can Stop Lettuce Killing You

In the winter of 2018, 210 people across 36 states in the USA and Canada developed fever, confusion, seizures and bleeding for unknown reasons. 96 people were hospitalised and 27 developed kidney failure. The youngest person affected was 1, the oldest 88. There were 5 deaths reported from Arkansas, California, Minnesota (2) and New York.

The Canadian Public Health Agency conducted a three-month investigation into what caused 96 otherwise healthy people to develop these bizarre symptoms. Via a survey, they discovered that 83% of those affected had consumed Romaine lettuce in the week before they became ill. Using trackback data from the Food and Drug

Administration (FDA), investigators were able to isolate a specific farm that, it turned out, took water from a nearby reservoir containing dangerous levels of E. Coli bacteria.

An investigation of this kind can potentially involve thousands of hours of work and millions of dollars. The investigators were racing against the clock to discover what was causing the outbreak and, more importantly, how to stop it.

Now imagine if every single head or bag of lettuce had been tagged with a unique code (like a barcode) that enabled investigators to access its complete history, saved on a blockchain. The data could include date planted, date harvested, where harvested and by whom, growing conditions (temperature, watering), when packaged by whom and where, when shipped and by whom and where, shipping conditions and so on all the way to the end consumer. Had this been the case, it would have taken just seconds to scan the code and check any of this data. The investigation could have been over within days rather than months, potentially saving lives. The investigators did a great job, but they didn't have the benefits of efficient and effective blockchain technology.

The Double Spend Problem

For cryptocurrencies, blockchain technology solves the problem of transferring value, and not just information, by eliminating something called the 'double spend' problem.

Suppose you want to buy this book with some tokens of a digital currency. The seller would need to know two things: that the currency you are paying with exists and that it has genuine value, meaning they can give it to someone else in a later transaction. If you pay using a digital currency that does *not* use blockchain technology, the seller can't be sure of these things. For example, you might have used the tokens for something else immediately prior to purchasing this book and, therefore, the tokens don't actually exist or have any real value.

Some stores and supermarkets offer a loyalty card system, such as 'Nectar' or 'Clubcard', that allow customers to acquire 'points'. These are good examples of digital tokens that do not use a blockchain.

To prevent fraud, supermarkets have to pursue one of two options. They either have to distribute physical vouchers that can only be redeemed once or set up a system to monitor each user's balance like a credit or debit card. Both options involve considerable expense for the retailer, either in terms of printing and posting the vouchers or running the technological infrastructure (servers, programming, data processing) behind the loyalty scheme.

These systems, for all their considerable expense, are not perfect. There are frequent instances of fraud, leaving the card holder with a negative balance of points with little or no explanation. The double-spend problem is solved in the same way that a bank solves the problem for fiat currency: with costly insurance.

Running these loyalty schemes calls for a massive investment of capital. In the USA, in 2014, the capital invested in loyalty schemes was over $2 billion. This gets passed along to the consumer in terms of higher prices for goods. Without this expensive infrastructure, the points are worthless. Even with the infrastructure, they can only be used in one direction and in a restricted number of ways.

Blockchain technology solves the double spend problem and all the other problems associated with loyalty schemes and fiat currencies. It does this by being an open, distributed, worldwide, instantly updated, automatic ledger of all activity involving a cryptocurrency. There is no way to perpetrate fraud because every transaction is cryptographically secured and verified. In fact, each one is verified hundreds of times and continues to be verified long after the transaction takes place.

If you use cryptocurrency to buy this book, the blockchain ledger is updated as soon as you transfer tokens to pay the seller. This happens instantaneously, even if the seller doesn't receive the payment in their digital wallet for some time — as is the case for bitcoin transactions today. Once completed, the transaction becomes part of the blockchain forever.

Over time, blocks (representing a certain pre-determined amount of cryptocurrency) are added to the blockchain based on the generation of new transactions that are always searchable, traceable but also anonymous (unless you happen to know the address of a specific user, for that particular transaction). At present, for bitcoin, a new block is added for every 2020 transactions, with the processors taking their (minuscule and scalable) fee for processing the transaction each time. This results in a completely closed ecosystem in which both sender and receiver, payer and payee, have access to all the relevant information in the ledger.

What's more, the fees involved are tiny when compared with those of fiat currency transactions. This table illustrates the cost of transferring 1000 units of a currency (in this example dollars) using traditional methods verses cryptocurrencies.

Unit	$1000	
Cash	$10	$5 withdrawal and $5 deposit
Debit card	$7.50	Average fee is 0.75%
Credit card	$17.50	Average fee is 1.75%
Paypal	$30	Average fee is 3%
Bitcoin	$0.84	Average fee during 2019
XRP	$0.01	Rounded up

As you can see, cryptocurrencies are significantly cheaper and are *not* based on a percentage of the total transaction value. While the fee may fluctuate in line with demand, you will never pay a percentage of the amount you transfer. This obviously represents a huge saving when transferring larger sums of capital.

One of the amazing things about blockchain technology is that it has *no failure rate*. A transaction is only added to the blockchain if it is successful — it cannot *partially* succeed. If there is a mistake in the transaction instructions, the blockchain will reject it and the transaction will not take place. Due to the cryptographic encryption imposed by the blockchain network, the laws of physics would have to be broken for a transaction to be incorrectly processed.

If supermarkets switched to a system of rewarding loyalty based on blockchain, you would be able to collect a genuine currency that you could use anywhere and on anything (or invest, if the number of coins is fixed). In addition to this, the price of the goods you purchase would become significantly cheaper as all the computation and data mining would be achieved efficiently and effectively by the blockchain network practically for free. In the 21st century, we may find that loyalty scheme tokens start to replace fiat currency as the main method of payment in supermarkets. This will allow them to be more efficient, more competitive, yet less expensive.

Why A Price Increase Is Likely

If you have ever followed the price of bitcoin or any cryptocurrency, you may have noticed that it is constantly changing. This fluctuation continues 24 hours a day, 365 days a year.

The price movement reflects the number of active bitcoin owners in the market. If there were only 100 bitcoin in existence and the price was £100 per bitcoin, the market capitalisation would be £10,000. If I sold one bitcoin, I would remove the value (£100) out of the bitcoin market and cause the price of every other bitcoin to drop by £1 to £99 per bitcoin. The bitcoin would still exist, it just wouldn't have an owner. It would be held in escrow on an exchange waiting for a buyer.

The next person to buy my bitcoin might pay more or less than £100 depending on the activity of the market after I sold it. For example, if there were only one bitcoin and multiple people attempting to purchase it, the price might increase substantially. Markets are the result of supply and demand.

There are so many exchanges of bitcoin happening all the time that, today, it is an extremely liquid market. You can instantly buy or sell practically any amount of bitcoin at any time. Whether the price drops or increases, there will always be people buying and selling so anyone can trade with confidence.

If the available quantity of a commodity is fixed, the more capital that is introduced into the market the higher the price and vice versa. You can witness this with any major commodity such as gold or oil where the price constantly fluctuates due to the ever-changing factors of supply and demand (and the fluctuating currency the commodity is being traded against). However, the available quantity of these commodities is not (yet) known so traders must work with the best information presently available regarding the current or likely future supply. If you have good reason to think the commodity is going to be in short supply you can expect the price to increase, whereas a likely glut will see the opposite effect.

The less mature a market is, the greater the price fluctuations are likely to be since a small number of individuals can significantly affect the price via their buying or selling actions. In more mature markets (such as gold and oil), where ownership is more diversified, the actions of each individual have less of an impact on the overall price. This means dramatic fluctuations are rare and usually regarded as black swan events, which we looked at earlier.

Today, the market for cryptocurrencies is very immature. Significant price fluctuations occur frequently and, superficially, seem to do so without warning. As the market matures, it will be less susceptible to these dramatic changes in value.

Most investors, when contemplating an investment, falsely compare the market for cryptocurrencies (which is measured in years and not decades, depending on which cryptos you include) with significantly more mature markets such as stocks, precious metals, property and fiat currencies. These types of comparisons tend to make cryptocurrencies look extremely volatile and therefore risky (which of course suits the purpose of those who wish to protect the traditional, fiat currency systems). The traditionalist lens says high volatility indicates a bad investment, so more traditional investors shy away and dismiss cryptos as a fad or an investment for fools.

However, in terms of tradable opportunities, there is unlikely to be a *better* market to trade than cryptocurrencies, which are a *tangible digital asset*. Although each coin is a digital asset, it is 'tangible' in the sense that if you wanted to see the code corresponding to your coin, you could. Most investors do not realise that the cryptocurrency market is the only one in which you can directly purchase tangible digital assets rather than trading though synthetics or regulated (and therefore geographically limited) stocks and shares.

If you want to buy anything through an exchange you can do it in two ways.

The first is to use a 'Contract For Difference' (CFD) or an 'Exchange-Traded Fund' (ETF). This is known as synthetic trading. All you own is a document that entitles you to the difference in price between entering the investment contract and exiting it. The CFD or ETF can be for anything: a stock, share, barrel of oil, ounce of metal or even a unit of cryptocurrency. If it can be traded, it can be traded synthetically. However, if the company that holds your CFD or ETF goes under, your investment capital is likely to go with it.

The second way is to directly trade the underlying asset, which gives you a better level of protection than any government or regulatory scheme. Trading physical oil is messy and expensive. Few retail investors want to store and transport oil over a long period of time, so most oil trades are synthetic. Being digital assets, cryptocurrencies don't have these problems, so it is rarely appropriate to trade them synthetically except for very large, short-term or high-frequency trades where the parameters of ownership are not as important.

If you do invest in cryptos, don't trade synthetics as they are equivalent to fiat currencies — infinite supply with no intrinsic value. Make sure you genuinely own the pieces of code that represent your cryptocurrency. You can take other protective measures such as backing-up your investment and storing it offline for maximum protection, which I'll say more about in a later section.

Mining: Proof Of Work And Proof Of Stake

The cryptocurrency eco-system consists of two different types of cryptocurrencies; coins that can be mined (hence the term 'minable') and tokens. The difference is that tokens are not the product of mining and are known as 'pre-mined' — every token that will ever exist is available on the first day of its existence. Bitcoin and ether are examples of a minable coin. Ripple (XRP) and stablecoins are examples of tokens.

Mined coins are created by computers solving complex mathematical problems that take an increasing amount of energy to complete as the difficulty of the problems grows over time. In metaphorical terms, on day 1 you might have to solve 2 x 2 to get one bitcoin. Several years later you must solve 298715 x 647220 to get the same amount: one bitcoin. The point is that it takes a lot more time and energy to solve the more difficult problem. (The actual computations involved are far more complex than these examples.)

When a given block of transactions have been computed and the block is complete, a random number (called a nonce) is generated that is unique to that block. The nonce includes a timestamp and acts as a means of verification that the block has been successfully completed. Once the nonce is generated, the network validates the nonce from that block against the network difficulty and, if it matches, accepts it into the blockchain. While this block is being processed, the next block is already being worked on by the network.

The process of matching a nonce to the network gets more difficult over time. By way of example, from March 1st, 2014 to March 1st, 2015, the average number of nonces a computer operating on the bitcoin network had to attempt to match rose from 16.4 quintillion to over 200 quintillion. (I trust all my readers will know that '1 quintillion' is 1 followed by 18 zeroes, or '1 million, million, million'. It's a lot. For your next trivia quiz, 1 quintillion seconds = 31,709,791,984 years.)

From 2016 to 2020, the bitcoin network processed and paid a reward of 12.5 bitcoin for each block that is validated. This reward is paid to the mining computer that is quickest to solve a block across the entire network. After 2020, the reward is reduced to 6.25 bitcoin for each block in line with the halvening process (which I'll explain in a later section.) Each block has a processing time of an average of ten minutes resulting in a constant (but progressively diminishing) stream of bitcoin being created.

As we've seen, mining involves solving increasingly complex mathematical problems. At some point, the complexity of these calculations will become too difficult for transistor-based computers to solve and the mining will be forced to stop (estimated to be around the year 2140). This is one of the reasons why the total number of bitcoin cannot ever exceed 21 million — the problems become just too difficult to solve. This means that every mined cryptocurrency (with a 'hard cap') has a finite limit, and because of this, its long-term value is not subject to inflation. Therefore, the value of each bitcoin should slowly rise over time, just by virtue of the fact that it is a unit of an increasingly utilised finite commodity. This is in stark contrast to all existing fiat currencies which, as we've seen, only tend to *depreciate* in value as their utility (use by more people) increases.

This process of creating new coins is called a proof-of-work model. The creators of the coins are rewarded for creating a block of bitcoin (or ether) by being paid a fixed amount of that specific cryptocurrency for each block that they mine.

As each block is mined, the blockchain validates the transactions across the entire network. This keeps the network constantly updated and functioning, so new transactions can take place. Over time, the number of mining computers slowly decreases because the difficulty of the calculations tends to infinity. This increases the resources and energy needed to mine each block, making mining ultimately unprofitable for all but the most powerful computer systems as mining becomes more and more expensive.

This reduction in the number of computers actively mining is anticipated by the network, which automatically reduces the reward paid to miners in keeping with a fixed timescale. This keeps the level of transaction processing relatively consistent over time. Every four years — or, for bitcoin, every 210,000 blocks — the reward paid to miners to process one block is halved.

In 2010, for every block mined, miners were paid 50 bitcoin. Today, this number has been reduced twice, first to 25 in 2012 and then 12.5 per block mined in 2016. In 2020, the reward amount per block will halve again to 6.25 bitcoin and then again to 3.125 bitcoin in 2024 and 1.5625 bitcoin in 2028. This systematic reduction of the reward for each block mined is called a 'halvening' event.

Rewarding miners in the currency they are processing means that at no point in the transaction does any capital leave the eco-system. Instead, the system is designed to add value to the specific cryptocurrency being mined that enables the fees to be kept to a minimum. All this happens in an open and transparent process where anyone with access to the transaction details can witness the transfer taking place in real time. To an outsider, without the correct credentials, the transaction is kept completely anonymous.

Over time, as the number of new coins being created diminishes, there will be greater emphasis on processing transactions — known as a proof-of-stake model. Cryptocurrency users and investors will be able to contribute to the network by pledging their holdings of certain (previously minable) cryptocurrencies and take a cut of the transaction fees required to process each transaction. Because of the comparatively low price of cryptocurrencies such as bitcoin in the early part of the 21st century, the fees are minuscule. Over time, as the market becomes more mature and the prices begin to rise, the fees (when compared with devaluing fiat currencies) may climb — but they will never reach the astronomical fee levels of our current fiat currency system (see table on page 36.)

Ether is the most likely cryptocurrency to switch to a proof-of-stake model within the next decade, which makes it a very attractive investment both from a price perspective and as a form of potential passive income. By the time bitcoin switches to a proof-of-stake model (probably between 2100 and 2140) the price of one bitcoin will have greatly increased, making the processing of transactions far more profitable for miners than mining new bitcoin. This means that people with significant cryptocurrency holdings will be rewarded for owning and holding their cryptocurrencies and will, therefore, be reluctant to sell. This fact adds to the likelihood of a major price increase over the long-term.

Because the quantity of every major cryptocurrency (including bitcoin, ether and ripple) is finite, any increase in user adoption will drive the price up. There may be significant fluctuations that traders can exploit, but if you eliminate the noise and focus on the average value over a period of several years, you will see a strong, positive trend. It is this trend that supports a long-term investment for all the major cryptocurrencies (bitcoin, ether, ripple). You can see this for yourself in the simple diagram on page 79. Alternatively, see the more detailed 'Charts' tab on the website.

You can plot a positive long-term trend line like this for all major cryptocurrencies that have a significant market value, strong fundamentals and a high number of users.

It should now be clear why the major cryptocurrencies are likely to increase in value over time. Factors such as speculation, more capital entering the market and general investment euphoria (from predictable events such as a halvening process) all contribute to drive the price of cryptocurrencies up. When purchasing your investments for fundamental reasons, you are really buying into the adoption of the technology and the solution to a global problem that cryptocurrencies solve extremely well. Bitcoin, ether and XRP are the most likely candidates for a dramatic and sustained price increase throughout the 21st century.

With cryptocurrencies priced at their present values, the investment opportunity is similar to being able to buy into the technology behind the next Apple, Facebook, Google and Netflix (all rolled into one!) at prices as they were in 1999. Only time will tell for sure, but my money is literally on these cryptocurrencies currently being worth a lot more in the future as they approach their true long-term market value. I believe this true market value will be achieved in years to come, at which stage more people will want to invest in cryptocurrency technology because the market suddenly looks 'safe'. However, it will be too late to obtain out-of-this-world returns that only come to those who are willing to contribute capital earlier than most and support these projects when they need it most.

Profit Points

- Cryptocurrencies rely on blockchain technology, which is an automatically updated and secured ledger of every transaction across each cryptocurrency's network.

- The price of every major cryptocurrency is very low today due to the limited amount of capital within the market. Because cryptocurrencies offer strong technological advantages, and solve serious economic problems, more capital will be introduced into the market — probably at specific periods related to the activity of each cryptocurrency.

- Market volatility will diminish over time (at much higher prices than today). Early investors will be very well rewarded for holding cryptocurrency on a long-term basis by being able to purchase more cryptocurrencies with a lower amount of fiat currency than later investors.

The Halvening

In the preceding section we looked at the 'proof-of-work' model. This model only works correctly if three things happen during the mining of each cryptocurrency:

1. The mining becomes more difficult.

2. The rewards for mining decrease.

3. The price of the mined coin increases.

These three rules must be true for any cryptocurrency to survive long-term and become adopted for use as intended. The first two rules are necessary and sufficient to provide a basis for the third rule to apply. As the supply drops, the demand increases which results in the price of the asset increasing dramatically.

Bitcoin and ether satisfy all three of these rules. The first two rules are built into the system and the third rule follows as a consequence. Despite its recent drop from $20,000, bitcoin is up millions of percent since its introduction. As the size of the bitcoin network grows, it becomes harder and harder for computers to generate new coins and this difficulty is reflected in the total effort and resources the computers must contribute to create one bitcoin.

The rate of creation, known as the hash rate, is, in theory, maintained at one block every ten minutes. When bitcoin was first mined, the reward was fifty bitcoin per block which resulted in 300 bitcoins created every hour. Because of the halvening process, after May 2020, 37.5 new bitcoin are created every hour. This reduction in the number of bitcoin created over time will continue until the mining activity stops completely. There will be a grand total of 32 halvening events for bitcoin, one every four years from now until 2140. Because of the halvening and the increasing difficulty of the calculations involved, the penultimate halvening (2136) will mean that only one bitcoin is created every 800 years. By this point, most mining activity will have stopped, and one bitcoin will be worth over seven figures.

Because the total number of coins is fixed at 21 million, the reward paid for mining new bitcoin reduces according to this fixed schedule. This is to ensure that the number of miners is kept consistent as the difficulty increases over time. It's not feasible for someone to mine 50 bitcoin per block when the transaction size, and string size, become so large that a huge amount of computational work is required to process the transactions. This fixed schedule reduces the reward by half around every four years for each minable cryptocurrency. Each halvening event is also independent to each coin with every halvening occurring at a different time, based on when the cryptocurrency was first launched.

When the halvening takes place, many miners drop out of the system (due to the reward decreasing against a usually lower price for each bitcoin, thanks to the preceding bear market) which means there is a reduction in the fresh supply of the cryptocurrency. This reduction in supply causes an increase in demand and consequently a price rise. This immediately causes a small recovery in the number of miners because the higher price means mining becomes more profitable.

This is why cryptocurrencies generally go through a cycle lasting four years: three years of growth, which tends to gather pace until it reaches a spectacular peak, followed by one year of equally dramatic decline (around 80%). You can see a diagram of this effect on the market on page 63 for bitcoin from 2010 – 2020.

The last time this happened with bitcoin, excitement and speculation caused by the halvening resulted in the price escalating from $1000 to $20,000 over nine months. A small number of speculators buying a relatively large amount of bitcoin (relative to the size of the market at the time) caused the other investors to either buy more or run their profits (by refusing to sell). This triggered a market where buyers heavily outweighed sellers – a bull market.

From a purely mathematical perspective, because of the three rules stated above, and the fact that there can only ever be 21 million bitcoin, given an infinite amount of time one bitcoin could theoretically be worth an infinite amount — or at least many times more than its current value. This is in stark contrast to fiat currencies, which, as we have already seen, depreciate to zero purchasing power over time. This fact alone makes bitcoin the most powerful currency on the planet at the start of the 21st century.

For the record, as of 2020, bitcoin is the world's 40th largest currency by market capitalisation. However, it is the *only* one that is capped. The other 115 currencies perpetuate the myth of unlimited supply. For further information please see the 'Fiat' tab on the website.

Almost every other type of mainstream investment, such as bonds, stocks, shares and currencies can be created indefinitely. When times are good, these assets are constantly being created to satisfy demand. Because there can always be new shares issued or fresh currency printed, this means that the value of these assets inevitably deflates over time. This is most likely to occur when the economy fails, and these more traditional investments fall out of favour.

It's true that there are still opportunities in these markets, but none of the opportunities are as good as cryptocurrency investing for all the reasons I've covered in this book. The simplest reason is that the final quantity of the stock, bond or currency is not capped, which means they are inherently worthless as more can always be created to satisfy demand.

Because the profile of most cryptocurrency investors is high-risk, high return, they are constantly watching for a price increase. Naturally, investors want to keep their capital in the market and to push their profits in the case of a breakout. Incidentally, this is why most investors don't sell out profitably and become trapped in the market. They chase their profits to the point at which the market turns on them. Then they refuse to sell out and end up holding assets worth less than they started with. Worse still, they then lose faith in the investment and sell out entirely, taking a considerable loss at comparatively low prices. After they have sold out, they blame the market for *their* decision to exit prematurely on an investment that would have yielded a profit if they had shown a little more patience.

In 2140, the last bitcoin will be mined giving us a total of around 18 million useable bitcoin. (The total is 18 and not 21 million because the rest were irretrievably destroyed on old hard-drives or trapped in abandoned and encrypted wallets in the early days when bitcoin wasn't really worth anything).

Long before 2140 however, bitcoin will probably have become the number one worldwide currency. This is likely given that bitcoin is inherently deflationary, completely secure, transparent and effectively relatively inexpensive to use across the globe. Its value already surpasses the currencies of Qatar, Lebanon, Morocco and Pakistan. In fact, in early 2020, bitcoin equals the combined value of the bottom 42 currencies in the world.

Because of this almost certain growth in value, by this point we are unlikely to see a whole bitcoin being used very often. By the time it is the world's most valuable currency, each bitcoin will have the purchasing power equivalent to about $3 million in today's terms. Hence, most transactions and everyday purchases will use satoshi, each being worth the equivalent of about $0.03 today. By this point, the bitcoin market will have settled, and its extreme volatility will be a thing of the past. In fact, because of its unique properties it will be less volatile and stronger than *any* fiat currency that has ever existed.

Profit Points

- The halvening process is a very important concept for all mined cryptocurrencies. The halvening reliably affects the price action and helps an investor to determine the market cycle of the cryptocurrency.

- Not factoring in the effects of the halvening can result in a bad investment where investors buy too high and sell too low.

- The value of mined cryptocurrencies such as bitcoin will increase in 4-yearly cycles: three years of growth followed by a year of decline until 2140. The growth will always be larger than the last all-time-high and the decline will usually drop around 80% of the most recent all-time peak.

- Cryptocurrencies are already a huge part of the global financial system and their influence is only going to increase throughout the 21st century.

Introducing Cryptocurrencies

Cryptocurrencies are pieces of cryptographically secured digital code that represent value. Because they are cryptographically secured, they can only exist in one place at one time and are impossible to falsify. There are now many types of cryptocurrency that have far-ranging applications and serve a range of purposes. Currently, the top three cryptocurrency networks are Bitcoin (BTC), Etherum (ETH) and Ripple (XRP).

To help you to visualise the potential profit to be made from each of these three digital currencies, I have provided the expected return per dollar invested at the end of each section. For simplicity, I have assumed that the capital is already in the market (at the prices when this book was published) and will be held until 2025. Ideally, an investor would also trade to achieve even greater profits. These estimates, which are for illustrative purposes only, are derived from historical data pertaining to movements that resulted in greater profits than those I have stated here.

Bitcoin (BTC)

Bitcoin is the world's first publicly adopted global cryptocurrency. The first reference to 'bitcoin' occurred on 18th of August 2008 when the domain name bitcoin.org was first registered. For this reason, bitcoin could be said to have risen from the ashes of the 2008 financial crash which was at its peak around this time.

As is common with the first instance of anything, bitcoin is far from perfect as a turnkey solution for replacing the global banking system. Compared with some of the cryptocurrencies that have been developed after bitcoin, it is cumbersome and inefficient. It has also faced more than its fair share of the criticisms concerning cryptocurrency adoption, long-term use and viability as an investment. Even today, the payment protocol is plagued by major issues such as slow transaction speeds. These have been improving and currently average about ten minutes. However, a bitcoin transaction can still take 24 hours, based on the parameters of the transaction and the status of the network. This makes bitcoin not particularly useful for everyday payments.

Furthermore, despite its comparatively widespread adoption within the cryptocurrency world, it is not possible for bitcoin to become the cryptocurrency of choice as the maximum number of transactions per second is currently 7 (compared with 1800 for Visa or Mastercard). There are already plans to fix these and other issues, including practical technology improvements, but they will require a significant update to the system and take considerable time and resources to implement.

Despite these setbacks, bitcoin is the most recognised, publicly known and owned cryptocurrency in the world today. It is also one of the rarest, since only twenty-one million bitcoin can ever exist. This combination of popularity and scarcity means that during subsequent bull market cycles, when prices will increase dramatically, the eventual value of one bitcoin is likely to be close to $1 million. This being the case, it will become increasingly rare for whole bitcoin to be traded. Instead, people will use and trade with sub-units of bitcoin called Satoshi, each worth a one-hundred millionth of a bitcoin.

Bitcoin's integration with the world of mainstream finance has been hindered by its developer, who goes by the name (or pseudonym) of Satoshi Nakamoto. This individual (or individuals) has remained completely anonymous, despite international efforts to discover their identity.

Even more perplexing is that nothing has been heard from the developer of bitcoin since 2010, when all the digital currency's permissions and intellectual property were made open source.

Bitcoin's dramatic price fluctuations since then have earned it a reputation for being risky. These price movements have mostly been caused by investors who hold large amounts of bitcoin having a disproportionate effect on the market. Over time, this issue will become less of a problem as bitcoin ownership becomes more diffuse and not so confined to a small group of individuals. Today, you can buy a huge number of items online using bitcoin or even withdraw it from one of the thousands of cashpoints (ATMs) that can instantly convert bitcoin into a fiat currency of your choice.

Bitcoin is created via a process called mining, which involves computers solving progressively difficult cryptographic problems.

Computers are also involved in validating all bitcoin transactions and it is this validation that is the key to bitcoin's (and every other cryptocurrency's) security. We have already seen (in the halvening section, page 44) how changes to the mining activity of bitcoin can have a dramatic (and largely predictable) effect on the price.

For every $1 currently invested, bitcoin is expected to return around $10 - $25 by 2025.

Ethereum (ETH)

The Ethereum network is an intelligent distributed network of computers facilitated by a cryptocurrency token called ether. You can use ether to pay for processing time to complete tasks on the Ethereum network. Tasks completed through the Ethereum network are called smart contracts and there is effectively no limit to their variety.

For example, Ujo is a music streaming service in which the artist and listener are linked by a smart contract through the Ethereum network. The smart contract performs all the legal tasks associated with managing the distribution of a music track across 900,000 possible revenue streams, including the collection of royalties.

With current streaming services, such as Spotify or Apple Music, a track has to be played about 152,000 times for the artist to receive $100 in revenue. This appallingly low rate of payment arises from the music industry's extremely inefficient systems, which involve many intermediaries and layers of bureaucracy. A smart contract dispenses with all the bureaucracy. It performs all the relevant accounting with greater accuracy than current systems and for a much lower fee. When you stream a track, the smart contract automatically reimburses the artist without the need for any intermediary to ensure the correct payment is made.

Another example of smart contracts in action is Basic Attention Token, or BAT. This is an Ethereum smart contract that is attempting to revolutionise online advertising. Currently, a typical internet user is constantly bombarded by largely irrelevant adverts. BAT is a token that allows the user to collect a payment for their attention from content creators and merchants. Everyone benefits from this system. Users only see adverts that interest them or get compensated for their attention. Advertisers waste less time and money, build direct relationships with interested consumers and gain very clear market research regarding what is, or is not, popular in real time.

As these examples show, Ethereum is an autonomous network for building artificially intelligent programs that can complete a wide range of tasks automatically. There is zero downtime and no dependency on any one company, individual or entity.

One major difference between ether and bitcoin is that the number of ether tokens is not fixed - at least, not yet. The point at which the number of ether will be capped will be decided by a voting system across the network when the number of ether are no longer in significant demand. In theory, the number of ether could keep increasing forever. However, this is extremely unlikely as it would mean that ether is not immune to inflation and other issues that plague assets with no finite limit (see the problem with fiat currencies on page 13).

It is important to note that ether has been designed to have a finite limit. It is just not currently clear what this limit is, unlike some other cryptocurrencies, such as bitcoin, where the limit was determined with the very first block (called the genesis block). The consensus is that the number of ether will be capped between 120 and 144 million tokens. This means that ether is around six times more common than bitcoin.

Ethereum is also faster at processing transactions than bitcoin, with a block time of around 15 seconds as opposed to ten minutes for bitcoin. This means that an ether transaction can take place a lot quicker and more efficiently than a bitcoin transaction.

The individuals who run the computers that process smart contracts on the Ethereum network are paid for the processing in ether. For this to happen, each ether can be divided into units of one billion, called a 'wei'.

When you want the Ethereum network to process a smart contract, you are said to be the 'task instructor'. You allocate a level of priority to the task and this, together with the quantity and difficulty of the tasks going through the network at the time, determines the fee to complete that smart contract. The fee is set in units called gas, with one gas equalling one billion wei (called a gwei). A typical transaction has a minimum value of 21,000 gas or 0.0000021000 ETH. If you want your task to be completed more quickly, you can pay more gwei and your task will be prioritised over smart contracts for which the task instructors have paid lower fees.

The model of pricing for an ether smart contract is effectively identical to the 'surge pricing' model used by Uber and some other companies. The greater the demand on the network, the higher the fee (up to a set limit) required to compute your smart contract over a shorter timeframe. Conversely, the more redundancy in the network the cheaper the fees are.

Smart contracts involve a computerised protocol that executes the terms of a contract automatically and autonomously without any human involvement. The possible uses for smart contracts are almost infinite. Any contract that currently exists outside the Ethereum ecosystem can be digitised and the terms carried out - completely automatically - by the Ethereum network using ether to pay for the processing.

The House That Ether Built

Imagine it is 2030 and you want to relocate. You have a rough idea of the value of your property, based on what you paid for it, and you have seen another property you wish to purchase for the equivalent of $500,000 that you think you can afford.

You access the Ethereum network on your phone and use a smart contract application designed specifically for property transactions. You have a balance of fifty ether in your cryptocurrency wallet and each is currently worth around $3000.

You input some credentials (such as your name and address) and the Ethereum network searches both public and private databases for information about you. This might include such details as your age, sex, annual income, number of dependents, insurance details, credit history, phone activities, location data, social media usage, health records and so on.

While it is building an accurate snapshot of you, the Ethereum network also searches for information about your property: when it was built, the price it was last sold for, any planning applications or changes to the design, whether or not the house insurance is up to date with no claims and other relevant details. When these searches have been completed, the application has a clear idea about who you are and what your property is worth.

Next, it contacts the seller of the property and provides them with an offer based on whatever information the network has obtained about you and your property. This seller either accepts or rejects the offer based on this data. If the seller rejects the offer they have to provide a reason, at which point you might enter into a price negotiation.

When your offer is accepted, the Ethereum network provides the information it collected about your property to another buyer who may wish to purchase it, stating the asking price for your original home. In this way, the buying and selling of property (historically a very expensive and time-consuming process) can be achieved almost effortlessly in a completely automatic, secure, transparent but open-source environment.

You decide to go ahead and purchase the property. The price for the property that you want to buy is 230 ether. Your current property, according to the app, is worth 180 ether and there is a buyer willing to offer you exactly that. By pressing one button you can automatically transfer the rights and deeds of your original property to your buyer, and the rights and deeds to your new property to yourself and pay for the entire transaction in ether. There is a 'cooling off' period during which all parties can verify the network's valuations. The cost of selling your old house and purchasing the new one, with all contracts just as secure as if you had used a solicitor and estate agent, is $0.0002 (rounded up).

You may think this sounds too good to be true, but it isn't. There are very similar transactions taking place today, with houses being bought and sold through smart contracts via cryptographic technology. This is only one of the many possible applications of smart contracts. Imagine a world where car insurance, business transactions or even voting systems such as elections are completed via smart contracts through the Ethereum network.

The Ethereum network is in its infancy but has potentially unlimited applications. It is currently the most likely platform to become the default for smart contract operations, which is why some people believe the future of cryptocurrency transactions will belong to Ethereum rather than Bitcoin. They believe ether will eventually overtake bitcoin as the largest cryptocurrency by market capitalisation. In their eyes, the Ethereum network has much greater potential than Bitcoin, in terms of technological adoption, because ether is more than just a token to exchange value.

Currently, the Ethereum network supports thousands of games, applications and even other cryptocurrencies that rely on it for their operation. Unlike bitcoin, we know who created Ethereum: Vitalik Buterin from Russia. He has a development team constantly upgrading the Ethereum network and adding new features.

The next major development will see the network switching to a proof-of-stake model as opposed to the current proof-of-work model (see page 39). This is of interest to many investors and is likely to result in a dramatic increase in the price of ether. Effectively, users and investors who hold ether will be rewarded merely for pledging their holdings to help operate the network. This, in time, could be the catalyst for ether to overtake bitcoin as the world's number one cryptocurrency. If this happens, it would result in huge profits for any investor buying ether below $1000.

For every $1 currently invested, ether is expected to return $25 to $50 by 2025.

Ripple (XRP)

Ripple is a payment protocol that uses blockchain technology to process transactions quickly, cheaply and securely. It uses its own token, called XRP. One hundred billion XRP exist, making them around one thousand times more common than ether and five thousand times more common than bitcoin. The network does not involve any computation other than sending and receiving the token XRP though proprietary software called XRapid. For this reason, XRP is a highly specialised token designed from the ground up to replace traditional ways of exchanging value such as the SWIFT system that banks have used since 1973 (as described back on page 27).

A typical transaction using XRP takes around four seconds and the network can process more than forty thousand simultaneous transactions per second, far surpassing current credit and debit card technology by a factor of twenty. One XRP token can be divided into smaller units called drops, each worth one millionth of an XRP. At present, the transaction fee (which can fluctuate due to market factors or be increased automatically to deter dubious transactions) is ten drops or $0.001, regardless of the amount or distance involved in the transaction.

Some argue that XRP is not a genuine cryptocurrency because, unlike bitcoin and ether, control is effectively centralised through its developer, Ripple Labs. On the other hand, this has made XRP attractive to large financial institutions who do not completely trust the decentralised operations of other cryptocurrency networks such as Bitcoin. There are now over 300 financial institutions using the XRP token to undercut their competition in global currency transactions. This admittedly small subset of the global financial system includes companies such as Santander, American Express and MoneyGram.

Ripple Labs have been so successful at integrating their cryptocurrency technology within the traditional economic framework that they have been able to make an impact at the forefront of world economic policy.

The International Monetary Fund (IMF) has said on more than one occasion that XRP has the potential to succeed the United States dollar (USD) as a global reserve currency. In 2019, no less an authority than Mark Carney, the former governor of the Bank of England, said the world needed a new "crypto-like" currency to reduce the world's dependency on the USD.

In addition to this, Ripple Labs has a formidable number of highly qualified advisors, directors and board members. These include Yoshitaka Kitao, president and CEO of SBI Holdings, a Japanese conglomerate whose banking arm holds 4426 billion Yen ($41 billion) in customer deposits. Yoshitaka has campaigned for the entire Japanese banking sector (servicing over 120 million people) to adopt XRP as its default liquidity providing currency by 2025. Ripple Labs also have a strong board of directors which includes former banking executives and former board members of SWIFT.

Ripple Labs has connections with central banks and other government institutions who are not as hostile to the adoption of XRP as they are to bitcoin or other decentralised cryptocurrencies. The fact that Ripple Labs owns a cryptocurrency has helped the company to enter the world's financial systems almost by stealth since 2012. Financial institutions are attracted by the fact that Ripple Labs processes all the transactions through its own proprietary software and controls a significant percentage of all XRP tokens at any one time. The fact that Ripple is non-diversified and centralised leads some investors to believe it will fail as a publicly utilised cryptocurrency and merely become a corporate tool that happens to use cryptocurrency technology.

Because of its centralised nature and pre-mined design, it is not possible to stake the XRP token and all fees are paid to Ripple Labs rather than back to the holders of XRP. The XRP token is however, the most resistant cryptocurrency to issues surrounding inflation as with each transaction, a small amount of XRP is completely and irreversibly destroyed. This means that the number of XRP tokens in existence systematically reduces with every transaction, which is referred to as the 'burn rate'. The average burn rate is around 5000 XRP per day, meaning about 2 million XRP per year. Even at this rate, it would take around 25,000 years to deplete half of the global supply (100 billion) of XRP.

The fact that XRP is not a distributed token is having such a negative effect on the price that some investors are losing faith in the potential investment opportunity. However, XRP's fundamentals are, paradoxically, stronger than most cryptocurrencies that currently exist because of its unique qualities and strong support outside the cryptocurrency world.

The price of the XRP token is expected to rise considerably during the 2020s as it becomes more widely adopted within the global banking system. Estimates range from $10 to $100 per coin. If this price movement is achieved, XRP may outperform any other widely adopted cryptocurrency investment other than very small coins (commonly referred to as 'altcoins') that carry a significantly higher level of risk.

For every $1 currently invested, XRP is expected to return $40 to $400 by 2025.

XRP - The International Conglomerate Crypto

Imagine you own a bank that operates throughout the world. Every day, your bank transfers vast numbers of assets across the planet. Every time your bank transfers any currency to another bank anywhere in the world, it uses United States Dollars (the most liquid fiat currency on Earth). For the privilege of using USD, your bank pays Bank of America a fee: at least $25 for small transactions or 3% for larger ones. This fee is just to use the currency (which is, after all, just a number sent via the internet). Conversion fees and administrative charges may also apply. When the dollars arrive at the intended destination, they are converted to the local currency.

There are several problems with these transactions. They are unnecessarily expensive and can take a long time. Some transactions take days, especially if they occur on a Friday or over a national holiday at either end. What's more, the exchange rate can change while the currency is being transferred. This, in turn, can significantly impact the amount of capital received by the bank asking for extra reserves.

The list of problems goes on. As often as once in every twenty transactions, human error or a malfunction with the SWIFT network means that money goes missing or is credited to the wrong account. For this reason, there is a vast insurance system specifically designed to reimburse customers when these mistakes occur. This insurance system costs us all millions of dollars in fees every year.

However, your bank is now trying a new technology called Ripple, or XRP, specifically for these types of global transactions. A transaction of any size can be completed in seconds and, due to cryptographic security, errors are impossible so no insurance is required. Another benefit is that XRP doesn't involve several intermediaries taking a commission merely for using a currency. Transactions that used to incur thousands of dollars in fees can be completed for less than a cent (see the table on page 36).

These are significant advantages, which is why XRP has won favour with international financial companies. XRP completely supersedes the current global banking system and provides a safer, cheaper, quicker and more environmentally friendly alternative to SWIFT as it currently stands.

Some members of the international banking community are calling for XRP to replace the USD as the global currency for international payments. In terms of its fundamentals, this makes XRP one of the strongest cryptocurrencies to own and invest in.

This admittedly simplified example illustrates how cryptocurrencies make it possible to complete transactions more efficiently, economically and simply than the systems currently in use. You may think I am offering a 'straw man' argument concerning the frailties of the current global banking infrastructure. This is not the case. In fact, cryptocurrencies may be the *only* way to keep the global economy working in the long-term if all the fiat currencies, including the pound, dollar, euro and yen, cease to be economically useful.

You may suspect that cryptocurrencies will always be too volatile for the everyday purchase of goods and services. This is where a different type of cryptocurrency called a stablecoin, designed to have minimal volatility, comes in. We'll look at this next.

Profit Points

- There are a lot of cryptocurrencies that you can choose to invest in. The top three are bitcoin, ether and XRP (ripple).

- Bitcoin, ether and XRP are the most valuable cryptocurrency assets as they have the most capital and development behind them. This may change, but changes are likely to be gradual and obvious to investors who follow the cryptocurrency market.

- Though they may seem similar, bitcoin, ether and XRP are distinct and designed to achieve different things. Every cryptocurrency has qualities that make it good for a specific purpose. For example, XRP is fantastic as a liquidity provider but useless as a means of passive income.

- Understanding why a cryptocurrency exists should be the first step when deciding whether to invest in it. If it isn't solving a real problem, it probably won't survive in the long-term.

Stablecoin: The 'Halfway House'

Most of the criticisms regarding cryptocurrencies arise from their significant and often dramatic price fluctuations. On the face of it, these appear to occur completely at random. Today, these wild price fluctuations make it difficult to envisage bitcoin, ether or ripple ever being used to settle everyday transactions such as buying groceries. Fortunately, while it may take time for the majority of cryptocurrencies to settle down and achieve at a more consistent price, some have been designed to have minimal volatility. Appropriately enough, these are called stablecoins.

A stablecoin is a cryptocurrency whose value is pre-defined in terms of another currency or commodity — typically the US dollar. No matter how many investors buy and hold the stablecoin, it will always remain at the pre-determined fixed price, such as one dollar.

Institutions such as Facebook, JP Morgan and Walmart, among others, have announced plans to launch their own stablecoins. This will enable them to conduct transactions using a pre-mined token that, despite not being globally distributed (like Bitcoin for example), is in all other respects a cryptocurrency.

From an investment perspective, stablecoins are useful only to the extent that they can assist the trading of other, more volatile coins. Currently, the most prominent stablecoin is called Tether, which has a dubious history and is controversial for several reasons. One reason is that Tether Inc., the company that created the currency, is alleged to have so far failed to prove it has enough fiat currency reserves to back its cryptocurrency. If this is the case, it invalidates the security and asset-backed properties of the token.

Investing in stablecoins such as Tether for short periods is not usually a problem. However, because most stablecoins are backed by units of value from what we know is a failing economic system, they share some of that system's problems. In the event of another economic crash and global depression, bitcoin, ether and ripple have all been designed to *rise* in value or at least be far more robust than fiat currencies. Stablecoins, on the other hand, as they are backed by fiat currencies, can potentially fail to the same extent. Authentic cryptocurrencies have been designed not to be influenced by the correlational risk factor of the economy (which I will cover in more detail in the section on 'Asymmetric and Correlational Risk' on page 73). Bitcoin and ether will continue to function and probably thrive no matter what happens with any specific country, major economy or major currency. They are global assets with global interests.

Some stablecoins are backed by assets such as gold, silver or oil. It remains to be seen whether any stablecoin will survive over a long-term basis, given that these projects are backed by assets whose price can be affected by market factors that are neither clearly understood nor properly defined. The evidence suggests that non-backed cryptocurrency projects will outperform any stablecoin in the long run. This is because cryptocurrencies do not need to be backed by anything in order to be useful. In fact, non-backed cryptocurrency projects have more utility in terms of economic resilience than any cryptocurrency that is backed by units of a fiat currency or commodity.

Profit Points

- Modern banking is an expensive, inefficient and outdated monopoly with a stranglehold over the financial world.

- Cryptocurrencies are designed to exist outside of the global economic system. They are immune to, or may even thrive on, the economic stress of a stock market, currency or property crash.

- The United States dollar has become an expensive and unnecessary way to provide global liquidity and, in this respect, is reaching the end of its useful life. A replacement is urgently needed - one that is digital, global, fast, secure and cheap. There are many contenders.

- Stablecoins are cryptocurrencies that enjoy low volatility, as their name implies. However, they are backed by assets that are affected by movements within the global economic system. Stablecoins are therefore useful for trading but are riskier when holding for long periods of time, due to being backed by the fiat system.

How To Value A Cryptocurrency

Value and Price Are Not Synonyms

If you google 'Bitcoin price' you'll see its current value expressed in any currency you choose. This information is useful if you want to know how much capital you need to make an immediate purchase. Apart from that, present price data is essentially useless. In order to be genuinely useful, you need to know the potential value in the context of previous and future (or potential future) prices.

The price of bitcoin was at one point $0.10, which means an increase to $10,000 either seems like an extremely high price to pay for the same thing or, if you happen to own some, a phenomenal return on your investment. However, if you know that the price was $20,000 in 2017, $10,000 looks like an intimidating loss. Out of context, the price is just a number that doesn't tell you anything useful.

If you examine a bitcoin chart carefully you will see that the price has — if you negate short-term volatility — always increased over the long term. This is true of all the major cryptocurrencies including ether and XRP. It is even clearer if you examine the price action on a logarithmic chart (Figure 1), rather than a linear chart (Figure 2).

These charts enable you to see the long-term increase in the price of an asset such as bitcoin, as the number of users rises over time. You can use this to your advantage and buy when the price is contextually low against the backdrop of this constant price increase.

As more people start using bitcoin, the volatility will also increase so that each 'wave' of the chart will be larger than the previous one. This is illustrated in the chart overleaf on page 64. The boxes represent almost identical price action but the proportions are larger reflecting the growth of the market. This means that we can expect the *next* increase in price to also be proportionally larger.

This data suggests that, so long as you take the long-term view, purchasing bitcoin at any price below $20,000 is justified for as long as the adoption trend continues (i.e. Bitcoin continues to be a technology that people want to use).

Fig. 1: A logarithmic BTC chart all time

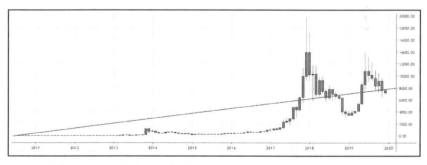

Fig. 2: A linear BTC chart all time

If investors knew with certainty that the price of bitcoin was going to increase to $500,000 over a specified period, things would be very different. None of them would question a purchase price below $20,000 (or even $400,000) because they would be certain of making a very healthy return. Every investor would be extremely eager to enter the market with all their investment capital. While it's true that nothing in life is certain, we can use data, previous price action and statistics to help us determine the most probable outcome.

When valuing new companies with little or no trading history (and, therefore, no agreed price), investors derive a valuation from what are called 'fundamentals'. We can define these as 'usually intangible qualities likely to result in the value of the company increasing or decreasing over a specified time'.

Fundamentals include factors such as the calibre of the directors or senior management team, historical sales figures and staff retention rates. If any of these are of concern — for example, if staff keep leaving because of toxic management — investors tend to avoid investing in the long-term growth of the company or may even bet

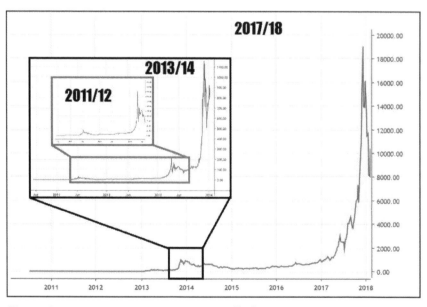

Fig. 3: Same price action, proportionally larger waves

against it. Thousands of analysts around the world, who pride themselves on their ability to value companies, are working with *less* data than cryptocurrencies can provide to the diligent investor. The investor just has to know where to look and what to look for.

Value investors don't tend to follow the latest fad in technology, fashion or entertainment. Instead, they invest in companies with strong fundamentals whose brands permeate the fabric of society, such as Apple, Coca-Cola and Microsoft. Value investors attempt to purchase their shares when the fundamentals are opposed to the price of the share or the dividend yield the company is offering. By holding the stock over decades, they plan on both the share price and the dividend yield increasing over the long-term, when the market increases the price so it is in line with the fundamentals (value). When the discrepancy between the share price and the value of the fundamentals becomes smaller, they may sell in order to invest in a new company with a larger discrepancy.

This is investing (which focuses on long-term potential and profits, over a timeframe measured in years) rather than trading, which takes a short-term perspective (hours to days). An investor only sells when they feel their investment has reached maturity and parity with the long-term fundamentals, rather than reacting to short-term price action caused by volatility.

Examples of strong fundamentals for a company such as Google would be the number of daily searches and whether this is growing or dropping. A strong fundamental of Virgin is a dynamic, ambitious CEO with a track record of success. Many fundamentals are subjective in nature but they can nonetheless help you to make good decisions, especially when a lot of information is not available or missing.

Investing in strong fundamentally supported cryptocurrencies is less risky than investing in new technology companies. Not only can you use fundamentals to great effect, but you also have historic price data to work from. By looking at the historical data, you can discover what a cryptocurrency was worth at any point in the past and use this to arrive at an informed decision. You never have all the data you'd like to have and it's never 100% reliable. Nonetheless, putting all the available data together can give you a better idea of your risk, expected return and potential loss.

Countless fundamentals could be relevant to the value of any given cryptocurrency and therefore affect your investment decisions. Here are the most important ones you need to know about and consider when planning your investments.

Market Capitalisation

This is the total amount of capital invested in the cryptocurrency at any given time and is usually, though not necessarily always, measured in US dollars. The higher the market capitalisation, the stronger the cryptocurrency. However, there is a trade-off regarding the potential for extremely profitable returns. The stronger the cryptocurrency market capitalisation, the more limited its upward potential tends to be.

Market Share

This is the percentage of the total cryptocurrency market devoted to the cryptocurrency. It indicates how much of the marketplace is adopting or using a particular cryptocurrency. In other words, it gives you a good indication as to how many people find the cryptocurrency useful. The higher the percentage the stronger the cryptocurrency. By way of example, Bitcoin is usually above 50%. Small projects with less than 1% of the market *can* still be worth investing in, but they carry a greater risk of long-term failure and loss of capital.

Transaction Volume

This refers to the number of transactions occurring within a given period. In general terms, the higher the number of transactions, the more viability the cryptocurrency is said to have. Low transaction volume doesn't necessarily mean a cryptocurrency is worthless. It may just not yet be widely adopted (though this could change). On strong trading days this metric can be deceptive. It's possible for traders to initiate transactions worth millions of dollars without using the cryptocurrency for its intended purpose, so this fundamental is only useful when viewed in combination with other strong fundamental reasons to invest.

Development Team And Update Cycle

If the cryptocurrency has a specific development team, who is the leader and what credentials do they have that would help to develop and strengthen the cryptocurrency? How many people are in the development team? It can be difficult to get good information about this fundamental for cryptocurrencies that, like bitcoin, have no employed developers but rely on thousands of volunteers instead.

Generally, the more experienced and suitably qualified the development team behind a cryptocurrency project, the more potential it has as a viable investment opportunity. You can also check how frequently a cryptocurrency project is developed and monitor its progress via a website such as GitHub. Projects that have not had an update for a while (months) may indicate that the project is performing poorly and are to be avoided as viable investment opportunities.

Partnerships With Financial Institutions

Does the cryptocurrency have partnerships in place with pre-existing non-crypto financial institutions? Furthermore, are these institutions supporting or using the cryptocurrency for its intended purpose and deriving a direct benefit? If the answer is yes in both cases, this is a very favourable fundamental. The greater the number and quality of these partnerships (for example, with a major technology company or financial institution) the more likely it is that the cryptocurrency will still exist in ten years and be trading at a substantially higher price than it is today.

Extent Of Adoption

Are people using the cryptocurrency to solve the problems it was intended to solve? Is it starting to fulfil its purpose rather than just being hoarded by speculators keen to sell out as soon as the price increases? Bitcoin is being used in genuine transactions every day; some other cryptocurrencies are not. If a cryptocurrency is unlikely to grow in terms of real-world adoption and traction, then it is likely to be eventually replaced by another cryptocurrency that does a similar (or superior) function with more real-world users.

Number Of Users

How many people are holding or using the coins? The more users a cryptocurrency has, the higher that cryptocurrency's investment potential. It's also worth asking if the cryptocurrency project has major support from 'HODL' investors.

A note of explanation: 'HODL' is a misspelling of 'hold' which appeared on the Reddit website in the early days of cryptocurrency investing. It has since come to mean 'Hold On for Dear Life' and refers to investors who will never sell their coins except to make extremely high returns. In theory, these investors would not only keep their investment if bitcoin returned to $1 but would buy substantially more. This practice contributes to a steady increase in the price of major cryptocurrencies over time as more and more people 'HODL' a particular digital currency. As previously discussed, this can be witnessed by examining the long-term charts of each cryptocurrency (see the 'Charts' tab on the website).

This list of fundamental properties is by no means exhaustive. There are many more that an investor could consider before deciding whether to purchase any given cryptocurrency. Not all cryptocurrencies have the same fundamental properties and any fundamental strength, which is always at least partly subjective, is constantly fluctuating. The key point is that the greater the number of strong fundamental properties a cryptocurrency has, the more likely an increase in the price and the less risk that you will lose your capital.

It is also worth mentioning that these fundamentals are variables - they can change during the course of a cryptocurrency's life. Assessing fundamentals is one way to evaluate whether a currency represents a good potential investment. However, some cryptocurrencies are all 'smoke and mirrors' and never a good investment. You need to know how to avoid these, which is the subject of the next section.

Avoiding Scamcoins

As with any new technology or investment opportunity, scams are unfortunately part of the cryptocurrency story. Investors have lost billions of dollars by believing scammers and not being sufficiently diligent with their investment decisions. However, before you invest in any crypto project you can perform some very simple checks that will increase your chances of avoiding the scam artists.

Is It Available On Major Exchanges?

While is it true that not all high-quality cryptocurrencies are available on all exchanges, major exchanges such as Coinbase or Binance are unlikely to list a project that is a scam. Naturally, the exchange has an interest in protecting its reputation and conducts thorough due diligence prior to listing a new cryptocurrency. If your potential cryptocurrency investment isn't listed on any major exchange and has existed for a significant amount of time (let's say at least six months), then you should avoid investing until you know more about it. At the very least, you will want to know why it isn't listed. (You can find a list of reputable exchanges by clicking the 'Exchanges' tab on the website.)

Is There A White Paper?

Every major cryptocurrency has what is called a 'white paper'. This is a document stating the cryptocurrency's purpose, who developed it and how. White papers are usually available on the cryptocurrency's website. For a good example of how a white paper is written and presented, look at the bitcoin white paper published in 2008 (see the 'Whitepaper' tab on the website).

Some sophisticated scams may include a (fake) white paper, but they are usually of poor quality with significant omissions and inconsistencies. The presence of a white paper is not a guarantee that the cryptocurrency is a good investment, or even that it isn't a scam. However, if the white paper is of high quality, verifiably authored by credible individuals and looks legitimate, this generally indicates that the cryptocurrency is a genuine offering and, alongside strong fundamentals, may have investment potential.

How Did You Hear About The Cryptocurrency?

If you hear about a new cryptocurrency via word-of-mouth or an advert, be very cautious. Some cryptocurrency scams apply multi-level marketing techniques in which a 'friend' (who may legitimately believe in the project) recommends the currency because they stand to gain something if you go ahead and invest. In effect, they are being bribed to give a positive recommendation and to get you to invest your capital by the scammers.

It's often said that if something sounds too good to be true, it probably is. This doesn't always apply to cryptos because some people *have* achieved phenomenal returns that seemed 'too good to be true' at the time (see the pizza example on page 8). It is more useful to look for inconsistencies in the business model or rationale of the cryptocurrency. For example, one of the largest scams offered its participants 15% returns per month for life. While achieving 15% profit in a month is certainly possible with cryptocurrency investing, yielding this kind of profit *for life* is not.

Profit Points

* Assessing the investment potential of cryptocurrencies is challenging but made easier by examining the fundamentals.

* The greater the number of strong fundamental properties a cryptocurrency has, the more likely it is to increase in price and the less risk there is that you will lose your capital.

* You can avoid most scams via research and critical thinking. Is there a white paper? Does the cryptocurrency appear to solve a real problem (ideally, one that you can witness)? If the investment return sounds implausible look for more evidence. With any cryptocurrency investment it is always best, when conducting due diligence, to triple check and check again.

* [T] Use the free cryptoprof valuation tool to find current data on cryptocurrencies and help you assess any coin's investment potential. It's available under the 'Tools' tab on the website.

Trading and Investing

There are two ways to grow your capital: trading and investing. These are not an either/or choice, as some believe. You can use both to grow your profits more successfully than you would using either method on its own.

Investing and trading are both valid ways of growing capital. Trading is active whereas investing is largely passive. Trading is focused on short-term repetitive profitability, while investing is about using long-term market growth to yield significant profits when you sell out of the market entirely.

If you're a trader, the value of any commodity depends on its price today compared with what you expect its price to be at some point in the future. Assuming the price goes up, the difference between these two numbers is your profit. Every trade starts with the intention to dispose of a commodity, which depends on the movement of the price (an increase in price for long positions or a decrease in price for short positions) at a point in the future. Shorting is where you sell an asset (which you may not own in the first place) to buy it back at a lower price - the difference between these two numbers is your profit.

For a trader, markets and commodities are merely a means to an end; a way to achieve a profit. Therefore, to a trader, the price and market capitalisation is largely irrelevant, but the direction and volatility of the price and the market are very important. For most traders, the aim is to make a 5% to 50% average profit per trade, with 70% of trades profiting and 30% losing. No long-term trader is going to have a 100% success rate. A trade generally takes place over a short period of time (days, hours or even minutes). Once a trader has taken their profit, they either examine that market again for the next trade or abandon that market altogether to pursue other opportunities.

If you're an investor, you buy and hold a position, or a portfolio (a range of positions grouped together), until it becomes significantly profitable. The timeframe for investments is usually several years. An investor only wants the price of the investment to go in one direction: up. Investors usually have a hazy or poorly defined goal of achieving a vague profit over a non-specific period based on factors that are very much outside of their control (for example, the health of the economy with an index fund such as the S&P500). However, these factors have a high degree of profit variance. If the stock market has a bad year, a lot of capital can be lost in something that felt 'safe and secure' for a very long time. Because an investment is usually measured in years rather than days, astute investors typically rely heavily on fundamentals and, crucially, where the investment is within its market cycle (macro growth/decline) at the time of making the investment.

As a rule of thumb, and considering variables such as investment size, investor experience and risk attitude, it is advisable to trade 20% of your total capital (in order to reduce risk) and invest 80% for long-term growth. On big movements which align with the market cycle, it may make sense to sell a lot of your investment and 'short' the market with your investment portfolio as if it were a large trade. It is vital to understand the risk/reward ratio if you want your capital to achieve as much growth as possible while also limiting your exposure to risk and, ultimately, loss.

Traders and investors look at the market from different perspectives. Both are interested in the price - particularly if it is low. If you're a trader, a low price reduces the risk and increases the probability of taking a profit within a short timeframe. If you're an investor, a low price allows you to be more economical with your capital and utilise it across a greater range of opportunities. The larger your investment, relative to the price, the more profit you can produce from price increases over the long-term.

I believe that most investors who want to make money in cryptocurrencies focus too much on the (admittedly exciting) short-term gains (trading) and neglect the underlying technological revolution (investing). This is to the detriment of their long-term profitability. Furthermore, they usually lack the psychological tools and skills to trade profitably, with most buying and selling at the wrong times because they allow themselves to be guided more by emotion than trading or investment strategies.

Taking the long-term view and investing in cryptocurrencies that are likely to yield profits for a considerable period is better. Long-term investing is less risky and more likely to be profitable than trying to chase the next big price increase in a cryptocurrency project

74

that will most likely die within months due to weak fundamentals. Investors also considerably underestimate the sheer luck of being in the right cryptocurrency at the right time and deciding to sell at exactly the right moment (which might only last several seconds) to yield a worthwhile profit.

Personally, I have been accumulating cryptocurrencies for several years which I do not expect to yield a profit for some considerable time. I have also been trading with a small percentage of my capital in order to add to my investment while prices are comparatively low. This is the perfect strategy to adopt with cryptocurrencies as they are one of the most volatile commodities on earth but, for reasons I explore in other sections of this book, also have some of the strongest fundamentals of any investment currently available.

Asymmetric And Correlational Risk

Traders and investors also tend to differ on their approaches to risk. There are two distinct types of risk, both of which operate for any investment. The type of risk that is favoured by most investors is *correlational* risk. This is where the value of the asset is highly correlated with something — usually the economy. We can see examples of these types of investments everywhere from stocks and shares to property. When the economy is performing well, these types of investments have their best returns. The problem is determining when the underlying correlate is going to alter and negatively affect the investment.

Correlational risk feels safe and comfortable most of the time. For example, if you invested in the S&P500 from January 2003 to January 2007 you would have made around 40% or around 10% per year. This return would have been gradual, predictable and intellectually justifiable - every time you checked your investment statement you would have made a little more profit. The same person investing in January 2007 and selling in January 2011 would have lost over ten percent over the four years and at one point been down over fifty percent in 12 months. This is because the correlate (the economy) was performing strongly with the first timeframe and poorly with the second. The investment was identical, the conditions of the correlate could not have been more different. As the price of the investment gets higher, the higher the risk of loss.

On the other hand, there is asymmetric risk. This type of risk requires the intrinsic value and price of an investment to be substantially different. This book is an example of asymmetric risk - it has used up a great deal of my resources that I may never recoup, but if successful, it will outperform a linear correlational investment of my time and capital (for example, if I were paid by the hour to write). Every single cryptocurrency project with strong fundamentals represents a low correlational and asymmetric risk profile. As the price of the asset gets lower, the less correlational and asymmetric risk.

But, to investors who are used to correlational risk returns it feels extremely unsafe and risky - after all, the price (at least over the short term) seems to be dramatically dropping over time, not rising. Cryptocurrency investments are more volatile and appear to not increase in value over the long-term (in reality, if you look over a long enough timeframe, they do — see page 63). The correlational factor for cryptocurrencies is not the economy, but the rate of adoption and number of users. In fact, there is a negative correlation between cryptocurrencies and the economy as cryptocurrencies are a perfect solution to the major issues facing the economy in the early 21st century (see pages 13 to 31).

Both types of risk affect all investments, and when prices are higher, the correlational risk will outweigh the asymmetric risk of cryptocurrency investing. At present, most mainstream investments have extremely high correlational risk and extremely high asymmetric risk. Cryptocurrencies have extremely low asymmetric risk and effectively no correlational risk.

The level of each type of risk is largely determined by the market cycle of the investment you are considering. As an investor and a trader, you are at the mercy of the market cycle, which is responsible for the volatility of the market and the opportunities it provides for long-term profitability. This is the subject of the next chapter.

Profit Points

- Are you more of a trader or an investor? Would you prefer to buy into a cryptocurrency and largely forget about it until it is in a large degree of profit? Or would you rather take an active role in your investment(s) and make more profit by also trading and taking advantage of the volatility?

- Both trading and investing carry risks. The risk of only trading is obvious: you could lose your capital in a bad trade. The risk of only investing is more subtle: you could miss opportunities to double or triple your investment without using any of your own money.

- There are two types of risk - correlational risk and asymmetric risk. Correlational risk is (generally) a lazy way of investing and is prone to black swan events that can wipe out a significant amount of your capital. Asymmetric risk is somewhat counter-intuitive and takes a larger amount of effort, patience and skill - but the rewards are a lot higher and worth the wait.

- [T] Take the free cryptoprof online test to see whether you are more of a trader or an investor and then work on your weakest area. Maybe you are too risk adverse and need to adjust your approach? Maybe you are inclined to take too much risk, which will hinder your investment over the long-term. See the 'Test' tab on the cryptoprof website.

The Market Cycle

Every market you might want to invest in operates according to a cycle. A very simple version of this cycle oscillates between two opposing forces: buyers and sellers. When a market is dominated by buyers it is known as a 'bull' market. When a market is dominated by sellers it is known as a 'bear' market.

It is relatively easy to detect which type of market you are in at any given point. With cryptocurrencies you can use the price action of the largest cryptocurrency by market capitalisation (presently bitcoin) to plot the growth and decline of the entire cryptocurrency market (in effect, treating bitcoin as an index of the cryptocurrency sector in the same way that the S&P500 is an index of the health of the economy of the USA). An idea of the market cycle can assist you in deciding whether you should be looking to grow your investment, as the asymmetric risk is low or taking as much profit as possible off the table because the correlational risk is high.

The last bull market for cryptocurrencies (2017) saw the top ten cryptocurrency projects increase in value by an average of 14,000%. Bitcoin, the cryptocurrency that was on everyone's lips at the time, was the 14th biggest mover at only 1300%! However, these movements were weak and measured over days rather than years. They were fuelled by speculation from investors rather than fundamental reasons or real-world adoption of the technology.

This speculation (and reduction, thereof) was one reason for the ensuing dramatic decline in prices of cryptocurrencies during 2018. Investors decided that either cryptocurrencies were on the decline for the long-term or that better opportunities existed elsewhere and sold out entirely. Those investors that didn't sell witnessed their investments drop by 85% in the space of a few months. Very few held on for the ensuing climb back up in 2019, having decided that enough was enough at an arbitrary point during the descent. It is OK to want to make a profit - but when you start to feel greed kicking in, it's usually time to sell.

All markets oscillate between bull and bear conditions throughout their lifetime. From 2009, the world has seen the longest bull market in the history of stocks and shares which is why the economy, throughout the 2010s felt, on the whole, strong and stable. During bull markets, investors tend to become complacent about their returns and assume the good times will continue for the foreseeable future and any reduction in the value of their investments will be temporary and quickly recovered. As the prices of their investments increase (and they smugly make more profit), the correlational risk gets higher and higher until a catastrophe ends the ascent in the form of a recession or depression. This causes a huge drop in prices (and, correspondingly, the value of investment portfolios) and affects all mainstream investment vehicles such as stocks, shares, bonds and property.

When this happens, the prices of correlational investments such as these drop much quicker than they ascended, and a sense of panic and despair is established across the investment world. Investors lose a huge percentage of their investment capital that took years to build in the space of weeks, the economy grinds to a halt as jobs are lost, government funding is cut, and the property market stalls.

There is a way out of all of this: hedge your correlational risk. It's important to appreciate that cryptocurrencies are *not* dependent on any factors outside their own eco-system. In fact, they often exhibit a *negative* correlation. For example, between March and September 2018, the S&P500 rose by 13% to new all-time highs, while bitcoin dropped by over 40%. However, it was a different story in May 2019. The stock market dropped by 7% while bitcoin climbed over 70% in the same period.

This means that in times of economic uncertainly or despair, cryptocurrencies remain largely or entirely unaffected by economic turmoil. In fact, they usually *gain* in value. It is safe to suggest that during the next cryptocurrency bull run, investors will witness an increase in prices caused principally by two factors. One will be speculators, of which there will be many more than there were during the last bull run (2017). The other will be confidence arising from the widespread and growing adoption of the technology behind cryptocurrencies to solve problems that hitherto had no practical solution. Since 2017, the development and improvement of cryptocurrencies has not stopped. In fact, it has accelerated, partly as a result of the profits and euphoria created by the price action in 2017, which led more people to realise the many benefits and low risks of the cryptocurrency economy.

The wider market-cycle within cryptocurrencies is largely dependent on the price of bitcoin, which itself has a four-year cycle due to its halvening process (explained on page 44). Broadly speaking, this means that whatever fundamental changes occur to the cryptocurrency sector or the world economy, both the price of bitcoin and the cryptocurrency market have historically experienced three years of growth followed by one year of decline.

The actual trend of bitcoin over the past ten years has been very positive, despite many media reports to the contrary. It becomes clear when you look at the average bitcoin price (the straight diagonal line shown in Figure 3 and 4) over a sufficiently long period of time. Investors can get so misled by the short-term fluctuations in price (which are a trader's dream) that they fail to appreciate the true long-term growth of the asset.

I hope, by now, you are beginning to see that cryptocurrencies with strong fundamental support are extremely likely to carry on increasing in price, for the foreseeable future.

This is true about every cryptocurrency that has strong fundamentals and a track record of growth. The timing is now right (at the end of the most recent bear market) to note the survivors (which, by implication, will be those with the strongest potential futures) and invest in them. These projects all have the least asymmetric risk against previously strong correlational risk - prior to them dropping from their heights in 2017. Remember, the intrinsic value for a cryptocurrency project such as bitcoin is stronger now than in 2017 when the bitcoin price was $20,000. If you have never invested in cryptocurrencies before today, you are a lucky 4th or 5th generation investor. In the next section, we will examine the generational effects of bitcoin and the consequences for the cryptocurrency market.

Fig. 3: A five-year chart of BTC, demonstrating its lowest, median and maximal expected value.

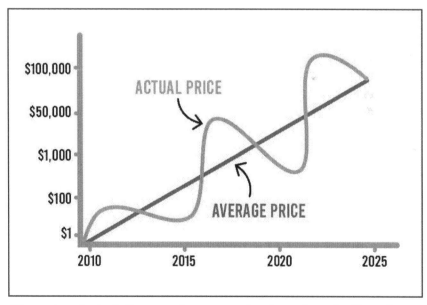

Fig. 4: A technical diagram demonstrating how the volatility of a cryptocurrency doesn't always show the full picture.

Profit Points

- All markets, including cryptocurrencies, operate according to a market cycle of increases in price (bull market) and declines in the price (bear market). These cycles are determined by the overall market pressure of the participants within the market (buyers and sellers).

- With cryptocurrencies, when the buyers outweigh the sellers, the price increases dramatically. When the sellers outweigh the buyers, the price decreases rapidly. There is a tipping point each time this happens that can be estimated to a good degree of accuracy, using technical tools.

- With cryptocurrencies, it is possible to pre-empt the bullish part of the market cycle by investing heavily during the latter stages of the bear market. This is usually when the market looks extremely boring and no one is particularly interested in it. Both the asymmetric and correlational risk profile for investing during this period is low, representing a good risk to reward ratio.

- Investors who purchased cryptocurrencies before 2017, rather than waiting on the side-lines, were rewarded for their efforts (or luck) by witnessing the highest return - averaging 14,000% for the top ten cryptocurrencies.

- You can use the attributes and properties of the assets within the market to help you to determine dramatic changes in the market cycle (from bearish to bullish, for example). One example of this is the bitcoin halvening process, which causes dramatic (and relatively predictable) movements in the price of bitcoin and the cryptocurrency market overall.

It's A Generation Thing

If you invested in cryptocurrencies between 2017 and 2021, you are a fourth-generation investor in the cryptocurrency market. If you have purchased your cryptocurrency within 2018 or 2019, you have bought into a bear market — one controlled by sellers rather than buyers. This is a good strategy for long-term returns but not for short-term returns (unless you are intentionally shorting the market).

It is a psychological struggle to buy long positions during a bear market as the price is likely to decrease for some time after you have made a purchase. An investor is faced with a black-box problem regarding when the price will stop dropping. No-one can predict what the lowest price will be and when the market will start rising in value again. This only becomes clear after the event, by which time it is, of course, too late to purchase at the ideal price.

The best solution to this problem is to use 'dollar-cost-averaging'. You start by making an initial purchase at any price low enough to feel comfortable. You then purchase more of the asset as the price decreases. If your purchase does not use any leverage, you can sleep at night knowing that no matter how far the price decreases, you are only getting a better price to enter another position to average down your investment. There is no risk to your positions purchased at higher prices. When the market recovers and starts to show considerable gains, you can decide when to take profit and repeat the process, if necessary.

As we have already seen, the market cycle for bitcoin (and therefore the entire cryptocurrency market) is related to its halvening process and lasts about four years. The bull market generally lasts around three years, during which the price increases exponentially in its final movements.

This is followed by a bear market for around one year during which the price decreases by around 80% before starting to climb again.

These dramatic fluctuations can lead the uninformed investor to think that cryptocurrencies are a risky investment. If bought in the latter stages of the bull market, investors tend to dwell on the 80% loss. However, they forget that it is only a realised loss if the cryptocurrency is sold — it doesn't even have to be a loss if you are patient and employ the correct investment strategy. Unlike other investments, it is usually better to stay in the market no matter what the price does by trusting the fundamentals of strong cryptocurrency projects due to the unique properties of this asset class.

When investors do sell out of fear, they forget about the growth that easily exceeds that of any other asset class in the world. This is not hyperbole. Bitcoin was up 150,000,000 percent at its all-time-high of $20,000. No other investment in history has delivered this kind of return or anything like it. Effectively, ill-advised investors focus too much on the price and neglect the fundamentals that are the true indications of probable future profit.

Bitcoin has the longest history of any cryptocurrency and is by far the largest cryptocurrency in terms of capital, so I am going to use it to demonstrate the generational effect of the cryptocurrency market.

1st Generation (2008 - 2011) $0.001 - $1

First generation investors are generally young, technologically sophisticated individuals who are unlikely to be motivated by profit. Ironically, these individuals are now the wealthiest investors involved in the cryptocurrency space. The early adopters of bitcoin are likely to have been politically and socially motivated to create a new form of currency that avoided all the problems associated with traditional fiat currency (and which were exposed all too clearly by the 2008 financial crash).

2nd Generation (2011 - 2013) $1 - $100

After the growth of bitcoin to $1 (a 100,000% increase), the price fluctuated significantly and took a further two years to rise to $100. Around this time, the second generation of investors became involved. These were more focused on profit and speculated on the price of bitcoin with intention of generating additional fiat currency from their trading. Numerous exchanges were established (some better, and longer lasting than others) and the market started to become a lot more liquid as the number of individuals trading bitcoin (and, as a direct result, the number of bitcoin available to trade) increased. Because of its pseudo-anonymity, the media started to run stories of bitcoin being used for illegal and morally dubious transactions on websites such as silk road. This is somewhat ironic given that every single crime in history up to this point in time had used fiat currencies and the traditional means of exchanging value anonymously: physical cash!

3rd Generation (2013 - 2017) $100 - $20000

With more significant price rises (to call the market volatile would be a significant understatement), mainstream media and institutions started to notice bitcoin (along with other cryptocurrencies) and referring to its extreme price movements. Most of this attention was overwhelmingly negative in terms of the adoption and use of cryptocurrencies. As the price rose, mainstream financial pundits were asked their opinion of cryptocurrencies and very few of them had anything positive to say. Here's a representative selection of comments:

> "If you are stupid enough to buy Bitcoin, you will pay a price for it one day. Governments are going to crush Bitcoin one day. There is use case for Bitcoin if you live in Venezuela, North Korea or if you are a criminal... great product!"
> — Jamie Dimon (Chairman & CEO, JP Morgan)

> "Bitcoin is successful only because of its potential for circumvention, lack of oversight so it seems to me it ought to be outlawed. It doesn't serve any socially useful function and this is just a bubble."
> — Mark Carney (Governor, Bank of England).

> "Bitcoin is a mirage, stay away from it. The idea that it has some huge intrinsic value is just a joke in my view."
> — Warren Buffett (Founder, Berkshire Hathaway).

Despite large institutions, banks and traditional investors knocking bitcoin, retail investors continued to buy, pushing the price above $10,000 for the first time. By this point, bitcoin had become a popular talking point and practically everyone who could afford to started to pay attention and invest. Suddenly, bitcoin was everywhere and had gained a level of validity among a subset of investors that very few investments ever achieve. A little over one month after breaking higher than $10,000, the price started to drop severely.

Ironically, bitcoin was being watched (and purchased!) the most when it was most likely to fall in value. Opinions were polarised. Some investors were intensely supportive of bitcoin whereas others were hyper critical and derogatory. When the price rose massively, bitcoin investors celebrated and attacked the detractors. When the price fell, exactly the opposite happened. You were either for bitcoin or against it, with both sides being highly disparaging about the other. This left the uninformed investor extremely confused about whether bitcoin was a glorious investment opportunity or a huge criminal bubble about to burst.

4th Generation (2017 - 2021)

The number of people who have heard about bitcoin has reached an all-time high — even if most opinions are based on myth and rumour rather than facts. The number of people who have invested in bitcoin or hold a bitcoin wallet is also at an all-time high. Bitcoin and other cryptocurrencies have never been more accessible and the interest from larger financial institutions has never been higher.

Because of the price action and subsequent sell-off, the number of interested parties willing to expose capital to the market is also high, though paradoxically not as high as when bitcoin rose above $10,000 for the first time. As of the start of 2020, there are businesses and infrastructure in place to purchase goods using bitcoin and other cryptocurrencies, involving either instant conversions to cash (via a bitcoin cash machine) or a debit card service such as Revolut.

In 2019, a movement by Intercontinental Exchange (owner of the New York Stock Exchange, alongside 22 other mainstream markets) launched the words first SEC-approved cryptocurrency futures exchange called Bakkt, its declared aim being "to expand access to the global economy by building trust in and unlocking the value of digital assets". This capital will almost exclusively be used to purchase bitcoin, ether and ripple, causing the prices of these assets to increase dramatically as the market expands through institutional investors for the first time.

The number of investors interested in the cryptocurrency market has increased the liquidity so much that anyone can confidently buy and sell bitcoin, ether and ripple without any issues. Furthermore, with the development of cryptocurrency synthetics such as CFDs (Contracts for Difference) it is now easier than ever to speculate on the price of cryptocurrencies without owning any coins or even setting up a cryptocurrency wallet. This arrangement suits investors who are not concerned about the long-term security of their investment when trading through synthetic investments (refer to page 39 for more details).

This situation is highly attractive to institutional investors who want to make short-term trades without having to physically trade the underlying asset (which can result in liquidity issues, slippage, insurance and other costs they'd prefer to avoid). However, due to economic uncertainty, it will be the investors who are holding and trading the genuine asset who will keep their cryptocurrency holdings when the inevitable global economic recession eventually occurs. After all, synthetic contracts rely on the company behind the contract remaining operational, which may not be the case during a global economic recession or another currency, debt or fractional reserve crisis.

The future looks brighter than ever for cryptocurrencies that solve real-world problems, have a large amount of fundamental support and are now backed by major institutions that can see and exploit their potential. Bitcoin, ether and XRP are likely to remain the most valuable cryptocurrencies for the foreseeable future. They present knowledgeable and proactive investors with an opportunity to avoid (and profit from) all the issues facing fiat currencies which are likely, at some point, to cause another severe economic crash of mainstream markets and products.

Profit Points

- Bitcoin (and other cryptocurrencies) progress in waves of ebb and flow which are linked to their development cycle, generational effects and properties.

- Keeping up to date with major developments can assist you in making the most from you portfolio and minimise risk.

- Cryptocurrencies have progressed a long way since they were first offered as an investment and now represent genuinely low-risk investments for sophisticated and knowledgeable investors due to their history.

Why Invest In Cryptocurrency?

Cryptocurrencies are one of the most exciting inventions the world has ever witnessed. The level of technological and economic sophistication involved represents a peak of human ingenuity. Normally, significant new inventions that solve important problems tend to attract significant investment. However, most investors will miss out on the opportunity to invest in cryptocurrencies because of one word: 'exponential'.

Each cryptocurrency market is capped at a finite number of units. What's more, the market is immature and undervalued compared with more mature markets such as equities or property. For these reasons, when any capital is introduced, the results are exponential rather than linear. To understand the implications, let's look at ten other investments you might have in your investment portfolio:

- Stocks and Shares.

- Bonds.

- Buy-to-let.

- Property development.

- Premium Bonds.

- ISAs / Bank savings.

- Precious Metals.

- Currencies.

- Emerging Markets.

- Foreign Exchange.

From a purely mathematical perspective all of these are *linear* investments. They are also correlational in nature with each other and the economy overall.

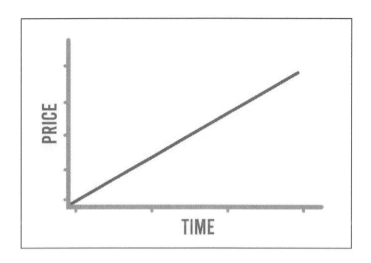

The graph of a linear investment looks like the example above. It shows that on average, over an infinite timeframe, the price of the asset increases by a small percentage every year. For example, it is generally assumed that the stock market will yield average returns of 7% per annum (during a year where the economy improves at peak efficiency).

To a hedge fund, pension fund or bank, this is a fantastic set of circumstances that creates confidence about investing in an instrument, such as an index, for several years. The bank and investor know that if the economy continues to grow, and there aren't any disasters, they will make a certain amount of money that is predictable and appears to be low risk. If bad times do come along, they will be temporary and investors who weather the storm for long enough will still make a profit.

This is why most investors tend to prefer to 'buy and hold' or 'set and forget'. Trillions of dollars are invested this way worldwide. Because disasters have been quite rare (1929, 1989, 2000, 2008), and the markets have always recovered eventually, it is widely assumed that these investments will increase in value forever.

Sure enough, the market generally doubles these investments over maybe 20, 30 or 40 years and the gains are, at best, 7% per year for good years and minus 5% for bad years.

The net result is a return that is comfortably above inflation, so significant capital such as pensions and company savings appear to be reliably invested with what is believed to be minimal risk. Some years are bad, some years are good but, provided the economy is stable and growing, you will generally get more out from your investment than you put in. This means that banks and savings institutions can offer investments that practically guarantee a fixed rate of return with what they believe is a very low level of risk.

The formula for this type of investment is:

Price x Time = Profit or Loss

On average, linear markets increase due to the number of people (and therefore, capital) in the market increasing, year on year. Another possibility is that inflation of the underlying currency over time makes the asset more expensive in terms of purchasing power.

This is one of the reasons why, in most developed economies, markets such as property and stocks and shares are currently very highly priced. The value of these assets is being fundamentally increased by investors buying and holding while continuing to speculate that the price will achieve a new all-time-high soon. This occurs while the underlying currency used to purchase the investment depreciates without fail every year, which artificially inflates the price of the investment even further.

New investors still enter the market and cause the price to rise even faster (while there are no catastrophic economic issues) leading to a sense of security arising from confidence that, no matter what happens, the market will always rise in value (barring the occasional dip caused by politics, war or trade tensions). This is called correlational risk (see page 73) and, as of 2020 with the S&P500 above 3000, is at its highest level ever.

Common sense states that nothing increases in value forever, especially something where there is the capacity (and profitable need) to create infinitely more units of value at any point.

At some point, there will be a stock market and property correction (just as there will be a correction with cryptocurrencies) and, given the way modern investments are designed, the next major correction is likely to catch most investors - who have seen over a decade of steady gains - out. Investors who have no idea that they can take a substantial loss will be forced out of their long-term investments with less than 50% of their original capital. This is the insidious nature of correlational risk. The larger amount of time between a correction, the greater and more dramatic the correction will be.

In 2008, the world witnessed the default response to disruption of the investment status quo: mass panic and hysteria. Investors sold (or were forced out of) investments they had held for years because the markets suddenly dropped and looked intimidating, unpredictable and terrifying.

What were these investors to do? They had to either sell out, take their losses and rationalise them, or become trapped in the market for a significant time (potentially decades) because they felt too afraid to take a loss and look for better opportunities elsewhere.

Those that didn't have the foresight or time to sell out of indexes such as the S&P500 (representing the cumulative market capitalisation of the five hundred largest companies in the USA, or trillions of dollars of investments from pension funds to government and corporate savings) had to wait eight years for their portfolios to return to the same level of profitability after the 'dot com' bubble of 2000, and then six years following the 2008 property crash. If investors were unlucky enough to not sell out of either event, they had to wait fourteen years for their portfolio to start showing good returns (assuming no further investments were made in that time).

This type of risk feels comfortable and safe as everyone is only focused on one direction and the declines are always unexpected and rationalised afterward (and inevitably recover, given enough time). On the other side of the investment spectrum, cryptocurrencies are an exponential market and asset class. This means they feel 'riskier' to the average investor, accustomed to linear returns from the slow and steady movements of an index such as the S&P500. In risk terms, cryptocurrencies are asymmetric in nature. If you invest when prices are low, and fundamentals are high your asymmetric investment risk is very low. Over time, when the market takes off, the asymmetric risk becomes higher making the market less attractive. The asymmetric risk for bitcoin at $1000 was a lot lower than at $20,000.

Most people find it hard to grasp the notion of exponential growth. An old fable might help to explain the idea.

The story goes that the inventor of chess demonstrated the game to the Emperor of India. Highly delighted by the game, the Emperor told the inventor he could have anything he wanted as his reward. It was expected that the inventor would ask for some incredibly lavish reward such as his own palace or large tracts of land.

Instead, he made just one modest request. All he asked the Emperor for was rice. Specifically, he turned to the empty chessboard and asked the Emperor for one grain of rice on the first square of the board, two grains of rice on the second square and so on, covering all sixty-four squares. The Emperor was amazed that the inventor had asked for such a humble and innocuous reward. He knew that he had large amounts of rice in storage and readily granted this 'trivial' request.

What the Emperor didn't realise was that it was *impossible* to satisfy the inventor's apparently 'humble' request. It would have involved more than 549 billion grains of rice, equivalent to more than 109 million kilograms.

This demonstrates the consequences of exponential growth. Over time, the growth increases not by addition or multiplication but by *powers*.

The formula for a market operating exponentially looks like this:

$$\text{Price}^y \times \text{Time}^y = \text{Profit}^y \text{ or Loss}^y$$

where y is related to the amount of capital entering the market.

For example, if the market capitalisation of a cryptocurrency doubles then y is 2. If it triples, then y is 3.

In the last bull market, the market capitalisation of cryptocurrencies increased by the 14th power. This is why the returns were so high and why the rule of asymmetric risk applies only to cryptocurrencies and no other market.

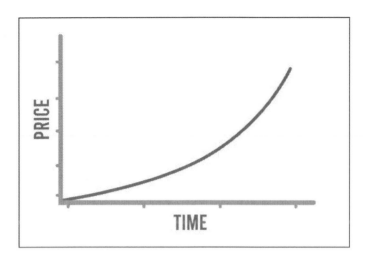

This means the graph of anything that grows exponentially (including cryptocurrency investment) is as shown above.

This chart is an oversimplification, a model. If we look at the actual chart of bitcoin price action in dollars since 2013, on a logarithmic scale, we can see a clear increase in the price while the volatility gradually diminishes. It shows that the minimum possible price for bitcoin as of 2020 is around $5000 with the maximum potential price being around $500,000 and $70,000 being the average expected value. (Refer back to Fig. 3 on page 79.)

Why does the cryptocurrency market grow exponentially rather than linearly? For a start, as we have seen at the beginning of this chapter, the market dynamics are very different for cryptocurrencies than for any other asset class.

The size of the market relative to other markets is still extremely small. In theory, the entire market (around 6000 projects or $200 billion) could be purchased by a large company such as Apple using just its cash reserves (which, as of 2019, stand at $205 billion).

The cryptocurrency market is currently much smaller than other markets such as property, stocks or currencies that represent trillions of dollars rather than billions. In time, the cryptocurrency market will catch up and even exceed the value of these other markets. This will happen merely from cryptocurrencies becoming more recognised as a viable investment where capital is diversified out of overinflated and overvalued markets such as property and stocks and shares. Investors who are prudent enough to buy prior to this public realisation, or tipping point, will benefit from the unique set of circumstances that will yield exponential returns.

For example, if just the capital that is currently invested in the S&P500 were to switch to cryptocurrencies ($25.6 trillion) over the next 12 months, the price of one bitcoin would climb to around $930,000, one ether would be worth $19,000 and every XRP token would be worth $30. This may seem implausible, but the S&P500 represents only around 5% of invested capital throughout the world ($544 trillion).

In fact, the cryptocurrency market is one of the smallest markets available to any investor. Investing in cryptocurrencies now is similar to purchasing land or gold in the 16th century and being able to wait to sell them at today's prices. The prices of cryptocurrencies are still very much in their infancy due to the technology and adoption not yet being mainstream. The cryptocurrency world is moving at such a pace that you only need to invest for 5-10 years to get a return similar to what a more traditional investment would take centuries to achieve.

For cryptocurrencies to fulfil their potential, the market capitalisation would need to be equivalent to the dominant world currency. As we have seen, this is currently the United States dollar. As of 31st January 2019, 1.7 trillion physical dollars are in circulation. If we include electronic money (bank accounts, savings and so on) this brings the total to $10.5 trillion worldwide.

If the cryptocurrency market replaced the United States dollar, at its current proportions, one bitcoin would be worth $356,000. The dollar represents 62% of global fiat currencies, therefore there would still be plenty of room for growth if bitcoin completely replaced global fiat currencies altogether.

	Fiat Currency	Cryptocurrency
Transaction time	Days or weeks	Seconds or minutes
Error rate	4 - 6%	Zero
Cost per transaction	$25 or 3% of transaction	Below $1 (for any amount)
Value	Decreases in value over time	Increases in value over time
Control	Heavily regulated and controlled	Self-governing and automatic

We have already covered some of the major benefits of using cryptocurrency as opposed to fiat currency. As a reminder, the major differences are summarised above.

If bitcoin were equivalent to all currencies worldwide, one bitcoin would be worth $2,848,717. There are serious investors in the world today who genuinely believe that each bitcoin will be worth $10,000,000 within their lifetime. Their justification for this is that as the world's population increases, and the number of people using currencies grows accordingly, the Bitcoin network will be able to satisfy demand and grow to a stratospheric price that is difficult to contemplate today.

This exponential growth usually concerns investors when it should excite them. The issues surrounding an exponential market are usually short-term problems such as volatility and (at least, in the beginning) slow price growth while the technology gains traction. For a property investor, gaining or losing 20-30% of their investment portfolio in any 24-hour period is extremely rare and would cause great concern. However, as we have seen, cryptocurrency prices routinely fluctuate by these percentages due to the immature state of the market.

It is unfortunate that most investors have so far tended to dismiss cryptocurrency investing as 'too good to be true' or unable to offer potential gains on a par with their preferred asset class. Their mistaken attitudes and beliefs mean they will miss the best opportunities to enter the market. By the time they do decide to invest, the majority of smart investors will be selling and securing their exponential levels of profit in preparation for prices to start to descend again.

We have seen how the cryptocurrency market is entirely distinct from any other investment or asset class. However, I know that most of you will not be persuaded to invest your capital by the mere presentation of facts. The next section deals with the psychological aspects of investing in cryptocurrencies. I hope it will help you to get closer to making a considerable profit by challenging some of the incorrect beliefs and myths that surround this exciting and hugely profitable asset class.

Profit Points

- The cryptocurrency market has risen from nothing to over $250 billion in the past ten years. This is still a small market but far from inconsequential.

- The market operates in a cycle of peaks and troughs on both a daily and yearly basis that makes it seem unattractive to most investors who are used to correlational risk and not asymmetric risk. Most investors are too used to steady returns that, if you study them, are riskier than strategic cryptocurrency investing when global economic circumstances affect the correlational risk.

- Examining a long-term cryptocurrency chart such as bitcoin shows a long-term line of support that will always increase - provided the fundamentals of the cryptocurrency stay the same and the number of users continues to rise. Investors can use this to ensure their capital is exposed to the cryptocurrency market with minimal risk and maximum profit potential when the level of asymmetric risk is at its lowest.

A List Of Excuses

"It is difficult to get a man to understand something, when his salary depends on his not understanding it."
— Upton Sinclair

If I had a satoshi (one hundred-millionth of a bitcoin) for every excuse I've heard for not investing in cryptocurrencies, I would now be the proud owner of several bitcoin.

Most of these excuses are from investors who don't completely understand the cryptocurrency market and its potential. It is not therefore altogether surprising that they feel extremely intimidated by it.

I hope that by reading the first section of this book, you now have a much better understanding of why cryptocurrencies are likely to be one of the best investments of the 21st century.

Here is a (non-exhaustive) list of excuses I've heard for not investing in the most exciting asset class in history. See if you identify with any of them. They are intended to help you to examine whether your own reluctance to increase your exposure is due to a lack of understanding or prejudice based on fiction.

Can you identify which excuses are holding you back from additional profits?

- Cryptocurrency is too high risk.

- Cryptocurrency is too volatile.

- 'X' coin could go to zero.

- I don't want to lose money / trap money in the market.

- It's too expensive - it was cheaper yesterday.

- I don't have any funds.

- Cryptocurrencies are not regulated.

- I have enough of X and the price has fallen — why buy more?

- I am in (another asset class) — let's sell that in time and use the proceeds to buy more crypto.

- Cryptocurrencies have no 'intrinsic value'.

- I don't have the time to invest.

- Cryptocurrencies are not ethical.

- Cryptocurrencies are not tangible and will never replace traditional stores of value such as cash, card payments or gold.

Some of these excuses may possibly have some merit. For example, I would not expect someone with no investment capital to prioritise a cryptocurrency purchase over their rent. Then again, someone in this position is unlikely to prioritise and read a book on investing.

The slippery slope of bad reasoning starts with the view that investments in cryptocurrency are 'high risk', 'volatile' or 'unregulated'. These weak excuses fundamentally miss the point of investing in these markets. Volatility is *why* speculators trade in the first place, since it presents opportunities to grow your account for free! If you would prefer to buy and hold (in other words, to invest), this is a start, but by trading according to a strict methodology you can get your capital to work as hard for you as you want. This helps you to gain additional profits when the market works with your investment strategy over the long-term.

Toward the end of this book, I have provided a range of free tools to help you calculate whether you have enough capital to achieve what you want from your cryptocurrency investments. These tools will also help you identify capital that is currently underperforming in other investments when compared with cryptocurrency's potential. **Please note that the recommendations made do not constitute financial advice and your individual circumstances may mean that the outcome of the assessment is not appropriate**. I recommend that you always gather as much information as possible and seek independent advice from a range of experts (but, crucially make your own mind up!) before altering a long-term investment plan.

As a responsible author, I feel it is my duty to ensure that, despite recommending that you take the opportunities in cryptocurrency seriously, you don't take huge risks with your life savings and ultimately lose them. If you do decide to make an investment based on the arguments made in this book, please ensure that if you were to lose the capital you have invested, this would not affect your overall quality of life or the lives of your dependents. **Remember, your capital is at risk with any investment**. If you manage and mitigate that risk, then you're likely to make a profit. However, this is not guaranteed.

1. Crypto Is Too High Risk / Too Volatile

As a trader, you want any commodity you trade to be as volatile as possible. The lower the volatility, the fewer opportunities that exist for making a profit. The belief that volatility is negative seems to stem from the mainstream media who use 'volatility' as a synonym for 'loss' or prices moving negatively against long positions — usually in investments such as the S&P500 that we saw in the preceding chapter. The alarming adjective 'volatile' gets applied to any market that is trading negatively at any given moment. It is usually implied that as soon as the 'volatility' (or negativity) ends, the market will return your investment to profit and continue higher.

This is wrong. Volatility simply means that the price is moving relative to another asset. Usually, that asset is a fiat currency such as the pound, euro or dollar. If the price moves the way that you want it to, then volatility is exciting and profitable. If the price moves against your position, then you need to have a contingency plan. When trading, the standard practice is to increase your exposure if the analysis behind the trade has become stronger as a result of the volatility. Conversely, you could cut your positions at a small loss, depending on the fundamentals and the market conditions at the time of that particular trade.

When trading in volatile markets, it is a good idea to use all the tools available to you such as stop-losses and an appropriate level of leverage, in order to extract as much profit as possible. Prices fluctuate constantly due to a range of random factors that are largely impossible to completely predict. As a trader, the market and volatility of an asset should be seen as a constant stream of opportunities to own a commodity or contract at a certain price and an option to dispose of it at a different price. The idea is to keep the difference between the two prices as a profit which enables you to increase your investment over the long-term and compound your profits.

When you invest into a market, you can only use the fundamentals and technical information available at the time of purchase to inform your decision.

Before you enter the market with your capital, it is a good idea to make sure you have accommodated and planned for any possible changes to the trade or investment. Your role as a trader is to interpret the market, using tools and data, and forecast a range of possibilities as to where the price is likely to move (usually over several different timeframes). When you have generated a trade hypothesis you can then enter positions accordingly. If your trade hypothesis is correct, you can terminate the position and capture the profit. If your hypothesis proves to be incorrect, you must be prepared to alter your position factors (reduce leverage or move your stop-loss) or kill the trade in order to preserve as much capital as possible for use in a subsequent and hopefully more profitable trades.

As a trader, you can reduce your overall risk by having multiple small positions within the same market, which is why dollar-cost-averaging works so well.

This strategy gives you more flexibility, but also requires more capital and resources to manage appropriately. The more positions you have, the more profits you can take while still having exposure to the market if something unexpected were to occur. You can use a range of tools to determine when probability suggests you should be taking profit out of the market. However, it's possible that the market could move beyond this price further, resulting in a profit taken too soon. As a rule, you should never buy all-in - always leave capital spare to buy more if the price moves lower - and never sell all-out (the price could move higher). This strategy ensures that whatever happens, you are likely to get better returns as you are still capturing something from the market but not leaving yourself totally unexposed, whatever the volatility or price movement.

2. Coin X Could Go To Zero

As of 2020, there are over 6000 cryptocurrency projects, most of which will not survive long term. Most of the smaller cryptocurrencies will fail (or have already done so) and all the money invested in them will be lost as the project value crashes to zero and selling any investment within them becomes effectively impossible.

These cryptocurrencies are usually relatively easy to spot as they have no strong fundamentals that would enable them to be successful. Most of the microcap cryptocurrency world is dominated by these very small projects that don't really do anything and yet remain surprisingly attractive to high-risk investors. If you are inclined to lose money quickly, purchase one of these tiny market capitalisation projects on high leverage and wait for it to fall and fail.

Perversely, many investors are attracted to purchasing an investment for next to nothing and hoping they pick out a unicorn project purely by chance. Naturally, purchasing one of these projects in the hope of a successful return is extremely high risk. If you insist on investing in extremely small coins, use very small amounts of capital (£10). Only invest in these coins with capital you are happy to lose completely — which is far more likely with these coins than for major coins such as bitcoin, ether or ripple.

If you are lucky and somehow pick the right project at the right time, you may get a good return on your capital. However, for solid returns that you won't lose sleep over, one of the larger and more reputable projects is where I would (and have) placed my money. There is a world of difference between investing in a cryptocurrency with a track record of only a few months (or sometimes days!), with hardly any users and no adoption, verses one of the larger cryptocurrencies with strong fundamentals and a solid track record spanning years.

Luckily, you can assess the probability of a coin being worth significantly more in the future using the same methods you would use for any security, company or investment opportunity. By using these tools and techniques in combination, you can more accurately determine the likelihood that an investment in a particular coin will have a positive outcome — provided you always sell higher than when you first purchased and the fundamental support of the coin is strong enough for a longer-term price rise (6-18 months).

If you adopt this approach, you know that if the price goes down and does not realise an immediate profit, the trade merely transforms into a longer-term investment that you hold until it *is* profitable. Without strong fundamentals, you have no idea of how likely the price is to recover to the level at which you made your original purchase, if indeed it ever will.

Let's return to the idea of a cryptocurrency becoming worthless and how unlikely this is for any of the coins with a larger market capitalisation (e.g. bitcoin, ether, ripple). For the price of any asset to fall to zero, practically everyone must sell the underlying asset and remove their capital from the market. This can happen, but it usually takes a specific and extraordinary event to alter the long-term fundamentals of an asset and trigger a mass exodus of capital.

Gerald Ratner knows this well. In 1991, he gave a speech at the Institute of Directors in front of six thousand people, with TV cameras present. He was chief executive of the Ratner's Group, best known for a successful chain of high street jewellery shops. In his speech, he decided to include a joke:

> "We also do cut-glass sherry decanters complete with six glasses on a silver-plated tray that your butler can serve you drinks on, all for £4.95. People say, 'How can you sell this for such a low price?'. I say, 'Because it's total crap.' "

He added that a set of earrings sold in his stores was, "cheaper than an M&S prawn sandwich but probably wouldn't last as long."

The media got hold of this story and it became headline news. In the furore that ensued, customers actively avoided Ratner's shops. The value of the Ratner's Group plummeted by around £500 million, which very nearly resulted in the firm's collapse. The infamous speech has become a cautionary tale for chief executives about the need to choose their words carefully.

Pushing a stock or security to zero is relatively easy, as there are always alternative investments (Ratner's competitors did very well out of the scandal). What's more, stocks and shares are unique — there is only one Apple with Apple's fundamentals, products, board of directors, management team and so-called 'intangibles' (such as the design and build quality of their products).

Cryptocurrencies are a completely different type of investment. They are global commodities with no CEO or shareholders (hence no-one to make jokes that eradicate their value overnight). Cryptocurrencies don't have the problems of a for-profit entity, such as one negative news story pushing the price down or one disappointing dividend causing impatient investors to pull out their capital.

With cryptocurrencies, investors are securing capital in a commodity that, given its potential adoption, could significantly gain in value just from routine economic factors. These include fresh capital entering the market and deflation arising from a small amount of the cryptocurrency being destroyed by its everyday usage (a deliberate design feature of some cryptocurrencies such as XRP to deter market manipulation).

One of the best ways to judge any cryptocurrency (or indeed any other investment) is to look at the total amount of capital invested in any one product against the overall market. The higher the amount of capital invested, the more the market is geared toward that product, and, therefore the stronger it is likely to perform against other products within the same asset class.

For some time, bitcoin, ether, and ripple have comprised over 80% of the entire cryptocurrency market, making them far more secure than smaller cryptocurrencies with fewer users. An investor can feel reasonably confident of a profitable return with any of these projects as they solve real problems and have a solid trading history, strong fundamentals and a large amount of capital already invested in them.

These coins are the largest of all cryptocurrencies (by market capitalisation). This means that the largest amount of capital, and the greatest number of people, are backing them. In fact, some analysts use the health of bitcoin as an index to determine the health of cryptocurrencies as an overall asset class. The likelihood of any one cryptocurrency becoming worthless is inversely proportional to the number of its users. Currently, each of these projects has had this many all-time users:

Bitcoin (BTC): 32 Million
Ether (ETH):   49 Million
Ripple (XRP): 1.6 Million

Naturally, only a certain percentage of these users are active at any one time. However, in terms of proportion, these three cryptocurrencies have the greatest number of active users and the highest rate of new users. Therefore, they have the lowest likelihood of their value dropping to zero. If anything, the value of these coins should increase dramatically as more people purchase and use the coins for their intended purpose.

It gets better. You can also use charting tools to determine the number of people who will not sell out regardless of how far the price depreciates. These individuals won't just hold their investment if bitcoin came down to a ridiculously low price, such as $1, but would actually buy more - and in the process, push the price back up again.

You can determine the number of people willing to hold on to their investment no matter what the price does by examining the lowest price of previous years. We saw an example of this with the long-term chart of bitcoin (see page 79).

As you can see from the chart below, for the price to go to zero, over 40 million individuals would have to sell their entire holdings, including 8 million who will never sell their bitcoin, no matter how low the price goes. From a statistical perspective, your bank is much more likely to fold than bitcoin is to become worthless.

Year	12 Month Low	Avg Mkt Cap ($)	Avg Nbr Wallets	Holders (est)
12	$4	1 M	30 T	6 T
13	$65	1 B	700 T	140 T
14	$200	7.5 B	2.2.M	440 T
15	$185	4 B	3.3 M	660 T
16	$365	12.5 B	6.6 M	1.32 M
17	$780	75 B	12.5 M	2.5 M
18	$3300	100 B	23 M	4.6 M
19	$3300	180 B	40 M	8 M

3. I Don't Want To Lose Or Trap My Money

Losing money is no fun, but to enter any investment and expect *never* to lose money is unrealistic. There are two types of losses: realised and unrealised. A realised loss is when an investor sells out of a trade or investment because something has gone wrong and (ideally!) looks for other opportunities to make their capital back. With an unrealised loss, the trade is ongoing but the market has moved against the position creating a temporary loss that will automatically be reversed when the price returns to profitability.

Unrealised losses are common with cryptocurrency investing. They are not a problem so long as the asymmetric risk is low (the position is orientated long and purchased near the bottom end of the market), and the investor can hold on to the position for longer than originally intended. Realised losses are trickier but *can* be an excellent way of trading (a stop-loss, for example, turns an unrealised loss into a realised loss because the unrealised loss has reached the limit of comfortable parameters within the trading strategy).

With cryptocurrencies at their current prices, the only way an investor is guaranteed to lose money, in bitcoin, ether and ripple, is if they sell their long-orientated investment at a lower price than they purchased it. Considering that cryptocurrencies are currently around 80% lower than their all-time highs, selling out at a loss should be avoided, if possible. If the price drops and you are patient, then you can allow your capital to merely stay in the market on a longer-term basis and take it out when the price appreciates, and the position is profitable once again.

In order to do this, you need to know three things:

1. The price is low enough (relative to prices at another time) to justify buying into the market now.

2. The price is likely to increase in the not-too-distant future to a level where you will be able to take a profit.

3. You are sufficiently close to the 'bottom' of the market (i.e. the lowest price within a designated period) to protect your capital from being forced out the market due to factors such as margin trading (if purchased using leverage).

How do you find out these pieces of information?

1. Look at an all-time chart of the asset you wish to purchase. If the all-time high is at least twice the current price (for example, if ether is priced under $150 then it is around 10 times lower than the all-time high of $1500), this suggests you should have at least one position in the market.

This is not to dissuade you from investing at higher prices. It just contributes to your peace of mind to know that many people have bought into this market higher than you are planning to. You are buying when the asymmetric risk is lower rather than higher.

2. How has the price moved in the past? What is the user adoption like? What does the order book look like? Are there plans for lucrative partnerships on the horizon? Does the product fill a niche that no other technology currently does? Are institutions becoming interested in investing? In other words, what is the fundamental news regarding the market right now and to what degree should you believe it? Remember, just because the fundamental news is either bullish or bearish doesn't guarantee where the price is likely to end up over any given timeframe.

3. What is the lowest price over the past market cycle? What is the difference between that price and the current price? Is the ratio large enough for a price rise to be more likely than a price decline on a specific timeframe?

4. Approximately where are we within the market cycle? Have we just had an extended period of bullish movement with traders running their profits and very little selling activity? Or are we at the end of a bear market where the selling pressure is weak, and the bulls are ready to take charge?

Reading the market and analysing the likely future movements of assets is a skill, an art and a science. It is by no means perfect and mistakes are common. However, as long as your interpretation of the market is better than chance (i.e. you get it right more often than you get it wrong), and you trade with a long-term outlook overall, it is highly likely that you will profit from your cryptocurrency trading and investing activities.

4. It's Too Expensive / Was Cheaper Before

From a purely technical perspective, when you are trading in a market to make a profit, it does not matter what the price of a commodity is. You still make the same £10 profit if the price of bitcoin moves from £1000 to £1010 as you would if it moved from £10,000 to £10,010.

When viewed from a trading perspective, where you are looking to grow fiat currency using a commodity such as cryptocurrency, you should not really look at the price and just look at the potential trade opportunity.

Of course, no-one thinks like this. Everyone wants to get their trade or investment at the best possible price in order to maximise the profit potential. However, if you get too fixated on the price, you risk missing out on opportunities to enter the market because you set your entry points too optimistically and, as a result, don't trade at all and therefore don't make any money.

As I said before, a good way to get around this issue is to use what's known as dollar-cost-averaging. You enter a (small) trade on the assumption of making a profit at the current price, but if the price depreciates significantly you can use additional capital to buy cheaper positions at lower prices. When the market does start to ascend, you can collect your profits on every purchase and be more profitable overall.

Bearing this strategy in mind, note that with any trading account you should try to remain as liquid as possible while also exposing your capital to the market at key points where a profitable trade is most likely. This means that as the price drops, so does your liquidity - but at the same time, with each position you enter, your potential to generate additional profit (when the market does ascend) increases.

Dollar-cost-averaging combines the benefits of a long-term buy and hold or investment perspective with that of a trading perspective. If the analysis regarding the trade turns out to be correct, you can take a profit. If not, there is no harm done and your position becomes more long-term focused while you look for another opportunity to purchase lower than your initial or earlier position(s).

At the start of this section, I said the price of a commodity is largely irrelevant for trading. You expose your capital to the market for trading purposes and (hopefully) build a series of (small) positions for long-term exposure to the market's growth. Some of these positions (most likely the ones at the lowest prices) you will keep and never trade with, as these will be the most profitable in the long-term and act as a hedge against the risks of future trades at higher prices. Ideally, you would adopt this perspective with multiple position sizes to have very small positions in the market for several years to benefit from long-term growth of the entire sector. These advanced trading strategies lie outside the scope of this book. For more information, see the 'Trading' tab on the website.

If the price feels too high, you are either concerned about trapping money in the market which could be better utilised or not thinking sufficiently long-term. Use the points I raised in section three (pages 104 to 105) to examine your thinking to see if this is the case.

If Coin X was cheaper yesterday, great! It might be more expensive tomorrow and if you are not in the market you may miss out on the opportunity for profit. If it was more expensive yesterday, great! You can purchase at a better price. Don't think as if each cryptocurrency purchase is the only one you are ever going to make. Each trade is one of thousands you'll place during your investment lifetime.

5. I Don't Have Any Funds

If this is genuinely true you shouldn't be investing at all. All investors should separate their investment capital from their day-to-day living costs and view their investments almost like a business or a company. If you are using this excuse on a regular basis, use the cryptoprof online budget tool (see the 'Budget' tab on the website) to determine whether you could free up capital from elsewhere — otherwise this excuse is usually a smokescreen for another reason not to invest.

Remember that with investments you get out what you put in. A 50% gain on a trade may sound wonderful if the amount of capital was $100,000. The same profit on a $100 trade is not particularly exciting. If you are not excited about the investments you are making, then why are you making them?

6. I Have Enough Of X, Why Buy More?

Your excuse might sound like this, "I have enough of coin X and the price has fallen so why would I buy more?"

Let me ask you a question. If the price of one bitcoin fell to $1 tomorrow, how many would you buy?

Here's a slightly different question: if you could use a time machine to go back to 2010 and I could offer you as many bitcoin as you wanted for $1, how many would you buy? How much capital would you invest? $100? $1000? $10,000?

Trading with the benefit of hindsight doesn't exist — if it did, there would be no market as every trader would cancel out every other trader. The next best thing is to prepare now for the next large-scale movement in cryptocurrency, which is the purpose of this book.

In 2010, when you could buy 10 bitcoin for $1, no-one knew for sure that bitcoin would increase to $20,000. However, today we know the market reached $20,000 per coin and that since then things have only improved from a fundamental, technological and, therefore, investment basis. The cryptocurrency eco-system today is one of higher adoption and usage, plus an increase in the number of people wishing to expose their capital in the market alongside a troubled financial system on the brink of collapse. This all contributes to a better outlook for bitcoin (and all major cryptocurrencies) than ever before. What's more, for all those reasons (combined with technical charting analysis) you know the price is highly likely to rise significantly above $20,000 on its next ascent.

If you are prepared to enter the market at a given price, then you should be more than happy to gain additional exposure if the price drops for a market reason (too much liquidity or a large short sell) and not a fundamental reason (a black swan event such as a huge change in market sentiment due to a technological or adoption rate set-back). Pullbacks and selloffs should be viewed as opportunities to either trade (short) or gain additional exposure at a lower price rather than as problems or the market not going your way. Provided the fundamental basis for investing in the market stays the same, fluctuations in price — no matter how large — should not concern you as a trader or investor at all.

7. I Want To Free Up Capital First

I talk to some investors who say they want to free up capital before they start buying crypto. If you're inclined to offer this type of excuse, try the following thought experiment.

Daniel has a tip on a new stock going public next week but thinks he does not have enough capital to buy it. He feels that it could be big and potentially double his money over a very short timeframe. He also has an investment in another stock which is under-performing. He believes the stock will become profitable eventually, but almost certainly not within the next week. Should he buy some of the new stock?

Not investing in something because you are waiting for capital from another asset is worse than saying, "I don't have any funds". It's worse because there is legitimate interest in pursuing the new opportunity, but you hold back because you're tied to an old opportunity that may or may not yield a profit. Psychologists call this 'loss aversion': being unwilling to take a loss on an investment on *principle*, rather than examining the situation at face value. This usually results in *greater* loss because you have the opportunity cost of not investing in the new trade *added* to the likelihood of losing on the original investment, which you know isn't going as planned. You are allowing an old opportunity that hasn't paid off yet keep you from pursuing a new, potentially better investment.

Using a strategy like this is an excellent way to miss the proverbial boat. As an investor, you want to have a diversified portfolio of opportunities with different purposes and risk/reward ratios. Waiting to sell out of one underperforming asset class or investment to take advantage of another (which is showing more promise) is leaving your exposure to profit to chance. It is a poor strategy and will produce more frustration rather than more profit.

To invest well, treat every opportunity at face value and without prejudice. Weigh up each investment and if your capital would clearly be better deployed elsewhere, pursue that opportunity. If you do choose to sell the original investment, a different way of thinking about it would be that you have been stopped-out of your original investment to secure the potential to produce a better profit elsewhere.

8. Cryptocurrencies Are Not Regulated

This is a common excuse for investors to systematically underexpose themselves to the cryptocurrency sector. It is falsely assumed by a large portion of investors that if an asset class is unregulated, it is somehow riskier than a market that is regulated. This is not the case.

Firstly, regulation does not mean that your money is any safer, more secure or less likely to be lost into the market. Here is a small selection of regulated securities. If you had bought any of these and not sold when the fundamentals altered, you would have lost all your capital without compensation:

Kodak / Enron / Blockbuster / General Motors

Lehman Brothers / Carillion / Reader's Digest / Toys 'R' Us

Maplin / Woolworths / Northern Rock

All of these companies returned significant profits for their investors on multiple occasions prior to collapsing. In the end, due to market factors, mismanagement and an inability to compete effectively, they all failed. At some point, the strong fundamentals that made these companies a good investment weakened and then vanished. Prudent investors would have noted these weakening fundamentals, withdrawn their capital and looked for opportunities elsewhere.

Cryptocurrencies are an entirely different investment vehicle to these or any other type of investment. You are not purchasing a share of a profit-driven eco-system. You are directly investing in and owning part of a new technology that is likely to revolutionise the transfer of capital on a global scale. The development of cryptocurrencies, alongside many other future blockchain applications that solve real-world problems, is only just beginning. This means that the opportunities to invest available to you today are extremely high quality with low asymmetric risk.

It is unlikely that cryptocurrencies will ever be a regulated investment product. The fact that cryptos are a global asset class (much like gold, oil or wheat, which are also not regulated) means that to attempt to regulate the market would involve imposing a geographic restriction on trading. If this happened, anyone in the

USA would only be able to trade under USA law and every other location would be excluded. This would be a legal and logistical nightmare considering that buying and selling of crypto is already happening all over the world (as intended) without needless geographic restrictions.

Regulated markets usually concern themselves with a security, bond or other financial instrument that has a natural geographic presence (USA, UK, Japan) and can therefore be regulated within that territory. Cryptocurrencies will never have this kind of presence. They are designed to *resist* top-down regulation of any kind. In any case, there is no need for regulation as they are intrinsically self-regulating and autonomous environments. Any further attempt at regulation would be inefficient, needless and counterproductive.

As we have seen, whenever anyone conducts a transaction with a cryptocurrency, a record of that transaction is validated and stored by the blockchain network. This record can be externally validated by anyone, including both the sender and the recipient, instantaneously. With today's fiat currencies, financial institutions such as banks carry out this validation on behalf of their customers. This validation involves huge resources, hefty fees and expensive insurance to cover mistakes.

Because all cryptocurrency transactions are governed by blockchain technology, cryptocurrencies are self-validating by design. The transactions are not only incredibly secure (more so than the banking system) but also automatic and 100% error free. Implicit regulation and automation means no management or handling fees, thus saving the end consumer (you and me) money and time. These are just some of the arguments for widespread adoption of cryptocurrencies throughout the global financial system.

What about the investment companies or exchanges offering cryptocurrencies: can they be regulated, and should they be?

A non-regulated market makes it difficult for any investment company or brokerage to itself become regulated. In an ideal world, the investment brokerage would be regulated to trade another asset class such as stocks and shares or commodities. This would mean that all trades are audited and monitored, communications recorded, and swift action taken in the event of an issue or problem.

This is known as voluntary regulation and identifies companies that are trying to offer their clients the best investment service against the unregulated competition. Given that there is unlikely to ever be any direct regulation of the cryptocurrency market and its operators, the best course of action is to educate yourself about standard investment policies and procedures and then avoid institutions and organisations that appear to go against these practices.

You may then face one final issue: because your investments in cryptocurrency are not regulated, they are not protected by any government remuneration scheme, such as the FSCS (Financial Services Compensation Scheme) in the UK. Fortunately, this is irrelevant. The FSCS is designed to protect your investment (and return your capital, up to a set limit) should the company you are dealing with cease trading due to bankruptcy or liquidation. You need to be careful as this protection only covers the performance of the regulated company you are investing with — it offers no mechanism for protecting capital lost to the market though any other means.

Investors should also note that when trading synthetics such as CFDs and ETFs, their capital depends on the company controlling the synthetic instrument remaining solvent. If the financial institution fails for any reason, then your capital is in significant jeopardy and is unlikely to be returned. We have seen this happen with Neil Woodford in 2019, where £11 billion of investment capital could not be returned to investors without taking a significant (70%) loss. This is the risk you are taking when you don't trade the underlying asset and, instead, trade a synthetic instrument.

As we saw in 2008 and during other times of financial crisis, when companies fold, they are likely to take investment assets with them, which is why the FSCS was created. It insures investments in regulated products with regulated companies up to £85,000.

This sum of £85,000 is unlikely to even cover your invested capital in *one* bitcoin by 2025. What's more, every method (unless otherwise stated) of purchasing cryptocurrencies that I recommend (in this book or on my website) ensures that you own the underlying asset and not just a contract. Because you, as the investor, legally own the asset, it cannot be taken from you if your exchange or brokerage collapses. By using carefully selected partners (such as Coinbase or

Binance) you can ensure that if your exchange ceases trading as a company for whatever reason, you still hold your bitcoin, ether or ripple (or your capital — which should be ring-fenced, if it is out of the market at that particular time).

It is worth mentioning that it's a good idea to store a large proportion of your cryptocurrency investment offline in a 'cold wallet'. This procedure offers the highest level of security for your investment and ensures that your cryptocurrency cannot be remotely hacked, under any circumstances. This contrasts with storing your cryptocurrency in a 'hot wallet' which, as they are located on exchanges and constantly connected to the internet, are vulnerable to hackers and phishing attempts. Quite a few (admittedly careless) investors have lost their capital in this way. If you need assistance setting up your cold wallet, read the guide on the cryptoprof website by clicking on the 'Safety' tab.

In addition, high quality exchanges have their own mechanisms for insuring themselves (for example, Binance insures itself with an escrow account designed for issues of theft, fraud or bankruptcy). This should give you additional peace of mind when investing and trading with a high-quality exchange that your capital is at a minimal level of risk of being taken from you via criminal activity.

In conclusion, with cryptocurrencies, your capital is safer invested in unregulated markets, where you own the underlying asset. Trading synthetic contracts through exchanges such as Plus500, eToro, Pepperstone, Coinbase Pro or Markets.com should be generally avoided, unless you are using these services in the short-term with the full knowledge that you own nothing by buying though them. For example, it is possible to purchase a cryptocurrency contract with a reduced fee through Coinbase Pro and then transfer the contract to Coinbase where it is then no longer synthetic but backed by a genuine piece of cryptocurrency code.

9. Cryptocurrencies Have No Intrinsic Value

The value of anything is constantly decided by the individuals within a market and nothing else. Value is derived from a mixture of speculation, adoption and use. Therefore, cryptocurrencies have more long-term value than fiat currencies as they are a tangible, self-regulating and automatic version of currency that are cheaper to use, more efficient and have no failure rate.

Here's another thought experiment. If you were to take a £10 note to Austin, Texas and attempt to spend it in a corner shop, do you think the local shopkeeper would be likely to accept it?

No? Why not? It is legal tender. It came from the Bank of England and is perfectly legal in the UK. However, the American has no use for your £10 note (other than maybe keep it as a souvenir) and therefore, it has little or no value to them. You may feel that your £10 note is worth £10 but to the American it is effectively worthless.

If you examine any commodity you will discover that there is no such thing as intrinsic value. Precious metal can become radioactive and effectively useless because no one wants to buy it. Property can become derelict and uneconomical to repair. The value of something is merely determined by the number of people willing to pay a certain price for it. Presently, the price of all cryptocurrencies is vastly lower than what they will be trading at in ten to fifteen years' time. This is mainly due to the immature nature of the marketplace and lack of adoption, which will only increase in the years to come.

Cryptocurrencies derive their value from their potential to transform the world of finance and produce a fairer, more efficient and transparent system for exchanging capital than ever before.

10. I Don't Have Time To Invest

Cryptocurrency investing can be a time-consuming endeavour. There is a steep learning curve before you can make an informed decision as to which investment is likely to be profitable. However, if you are prepared to invest in a market that is showing a low risk to high reward ratio, then taking the time to learn about cryptocurrencies will almost certainly be worth it in the long run.

I know people who have lost a great deal of capital in the cryptocurrency market simply because they didn't really understand the market or failed to take common-sense steps to protect their investments.

For example, consider the simple notion of keeping your digital assets offline when you are not trading them. This is the difference between having an investment that can be hacked and stolen at any time, and one that is more secure than your current account with your bank.

Just because you do not have the time to trade properly does not mean you cannot invest. Merely investing, by buying and holding positions in cryptocurrency, does not take a lot of time and the potential rewards more than justify the few hours it takes to set everything up. Furthermore, people who want to trade but lack the time or skills to do so can use the services of an investment house.

An investment house is the preferred option for serious investors who value a broker-client relationship with a firm that processes millions of dollars of orders every year. A broker within an investment house has the expertise derived from years of managing cryptocurrency positions for multiple clients over an extended period. This combination of time saved and peace of mind regarding your investments justifies the management and trading fees, which are added to each of your positions.

There is, however, nothing as good as learning to trade and manage our own positions. Yes, it takes time to learn, but the ends more than justify the means.

For more information on training tools and resources see the 'Advanced' tab on the website.

11. Cryptocurrencies Are Not Ethical

This statement usually involves one of three themes:

- Due to their inherent anonymity, cryptocurrencies have been used by criminals to purchase illicit goods or lauder money.

- Cryptocurrencies, by design, run on a network that constantly uses electricity to operate. They are therefore inefficient as a long-term payment solution as their carbon footprint is worse than the current system.

- My religion does not allow me to invest in products such as cryptocurrencies.

The media were largely responsible for creating the belief that bitcoin was being used to launder money, buy drugs and utilised in other illegal activities. Governments, regulators and banks were keen to promote this narrative because they saw cryptos as a business threat. It suited their purpose to paint cryptocurrency as at best a passing fad and at worst a sordid and ingenious ecosystem for assisting criminals.

However, there are several problems with this narrative. The currency with the strongest ties to criminal activity is not bitcoin or any cryptocurrency but cash — specifically the dollar. Every fiat currency is involved in illicit and illegal activities on a daily basis. This fact does not stop anyone from using fiat currency to purchase their weekly groceries.

It's true that bitcoin is a network of computers that must be kept operating all the time. It has been estimated that the bitcoin network requires 0.33% of the total global power consumption, or 73.12 terawatt-hours at its peak. That's quite a lot of juice and therefore a cause for concern, isn't it?

Well, how does it stack up against the global banking system? It is estimated that the payment processors Visa and MasterCard, combined, use around 100 terawatts per year to keep their payment networks in operation. Therefore, the bitcoin network (which, as the earliest cryptocurrency, is the least efficient) is around 26% *more efficient* than the current banking system.

Efficiency with cryptocurrencies is, however, largely a non-issue, as there are many other (pre-mined) cryptocurrencies available — such as ripple (XRP) — that enable digital transactions to be processed more efficiently than bitcoin in its current form. In addition, a recent study identified that 74% of bitcoin mining is powered by renewable energy, making Bitcoin one of the most efficient computer networks in the world.

Some people feel that using cryptocurrency or investing in it may be against their religion. For example, Islamic Sharia Law has rules about investing in assets that yield interest. However, in 2018, an Islamic scholar declared that bitcoin and other cryptocurrencies were permitted under Sharia law because the returns did not count as interest due to the number of coins being permanently capped (which, as you have seen is unique to this asset class).

12. Cryptos Are Not Useful In The Real World

It may surprise you to learn that you can spend cryptocurrency at any shop or restaurant that accepts credit or debit cards. Payment providers such as Revolut, among others, provide a debit card facility allowing anyone to spend multiple cryptocurrencies just as if they were using fiat currency. Not only that, but there are over 300 ATMs in the UK and 5300 worldwide — called Satoshipoints — where anyone can withdraw bitcoin for fiat currency instantly, based on the exchange rate at the time of the transaction.

Clearly, the everyday usage of cryptocurrencies is not one of its strong points with prices being as low as they are in 2020. Most people are investing in cryptocurrencies rather than looking to use them as a replacement for fiat currency. This is understandable, given that most people do not yet fully comprehend the economic risks inherent within the global banking system.

However, the adoption and everyday use of cryptocurrency is only going to increase during the 21st century. The volatility of the price of cryptocurrencies will gradually reduce as cryptocurrency assets gain more widespread use and adoption. With this adoption, the pool of individuals owning cryptocurrencies will become larger and more diverse. In time, cryptocurrencies will have the same volatility as traditional fiat currencies or even less, as they are global and not regional entities. At the same time, their level of security, transparency and efficiency, in contrast to the current global banking system, will become much more obvious to the general public. This will have the effect of increasing the size of the market many times over, yielding significant profits for early (4th and 5th generation) investors.

Profit Points

• When trading, never commit all your capital to the market and never sell all of your positions. All-or-nothing exposure leads to riskier all-or-nothing results.

• As a trader, volatility is your ally. Without volatility, no profit can be made. Don't allow volatility to cost you capital by taking too much risk with leverage, position size or reluctance to cut trades that have turned out, after execution, to be based on incorrect trading assumptions.

• If you wish to invest in very small cryptocurrencies (worth less than $0.01), only invest a very small amount of capital that you are completely prepared to lose ($10). Ideally, you should be using no leverage or margin trading, until the cryptocurrency has more fundamental support.

• Always remember to use fundamental analysis of any project you are investing in. The fewer users a cryptocurrency has, the more easily it can drop to zero.

• Know the difference between realised and unrealised losses. They are significantly different and understanding the differences are crucial to minimising the risk with your investment.

• Before deciding to buy any cryptocurrencies, answer the questions on pages 104 and 105 to discover as much as you can about the market.

• Try not to get too fixated on the price of any one trade or position. Remember you are potentially going to place thousands of trades over your investment lifetime.

- For price uncertainty, dollar-cost-averaging can ensure that you have some exposure to the market while meaning that if the price does come down, you can still take advantage of the lower price to yield additional profits in the long-run.

- [T] If you are concerned about the amount of capital you are risking in the market, use the cryptoprof budgeting and risk tool to determine if you are risking too much (or too little). You can find both of these tools on the cryptoprof website by clicking 'Risk' or 'Budget' on the 'Tools' menu.

- Provided there is no substantial negative alteration to the fundamental basis for investing in the market, fluctuations in price - no matter how large - should not concern you. In fact, these circumstances should be viewed as opportunities to increase your exposure to the market with less capital to make additional profit on a longer-term basis.

- Do not get emotionally tied to your investments. They are merely the tools to produce a profit and nothing else.

- To invest well, treat every opportunity at face value and not with prejudice. Weigh up each investment and if your capital would clearly be better deployed elsewhere, move it.

- Ensure that the exchange where you purchase your cryptocurrency is selling you the genuine asset and not a contract. This is not always possible for all types of trading, but your investment portfolio should enable you to own the cryptocurrencies that you purchase outright (and ideally move to offline or cold storage). Being diligent with this procedure will increase the likelihood that your capital is protected even if the exchange you are using does not survive long-term.

- For additional resources on trading and investing in cryptocurrencies, visit the cryptoprof website and click on the 'Tools' and 'Resources' menus.

Trading 101

How To Grow Your Trading Account For Free

To be as profitable a trader as you can be, you need to have an appropriate account size relative to your other investments or personal finances. This is to ensure that you can take advantage of as many opportunities as possible within the cryptocurrency sector. Only you can determine what level of investment you feel comfortable with, regarding any particular market, and this may change over time based on your individual circumstances.

One way to grow your account for free is by trading. When you trade, you take capital away from other people in the market who sell their positions to you or buy your positions from you (either in profit or at a loss). It is usually best to sell in profit (although not always) and buy positions as low as possible (or to sell as high as possible for a short) to increase the probability of you extracting as much capital from the market as possible.

There are a range of tools that can help you to assess the likelihood of the market moving in any particular direction. You can use these tools to establish the best price to enter and exit a trade. All these tools are based on probability and psychology, rather than hard science, and can assist you in testing your hypothesises to provide an outline of the potential price movement over a given timeframe.

A Very Brief Guide To Technical Trading Tools

Reading charts and determining the likely movement of markets is an essential skill for any trader. This book, along with the resources on the website, will teach you the basics of how to read chart patterns, look for trends in the price levels and identify opportunities to invest when the market is likely to move dramatically.

You can also use fundamental news, previous price action, support and resistance levels and the general market cycle to inform your decision-making before executing a trade. Any of these properties can alter at any point and as cryptocurrencies are a 24/7 market, keeping up to date is not an easy task.

However, a better understanding of how to read charts and comprehension of the basics of technical analysis can help you to feel more confident about trading these markets. The process of learning to trade never stops and there is always more to learn. Gaining experience by actually doing trades (when you have a basic understanding), even with a demo account, is the best way to consolidate and refine your learning.

There is also a lot of psychology involved in high-quality trading. As an investor, you will face numerous battles such as cognitive-dissonance, cognitive biases and emotions which do not help you in your goal to becoming a profitable trader. For this reason, I have provided an expanded list of resources on the cryptoprof website that can help you to deal with these psychological factors. See the 'Psychology' tab on the 'Resources' menu.

Long and Short

Every market is a battle between two opposing perspectives on the price of an asset. If you expect the price to rise, then you are long in the market. If you are expecting the price to decline, then you are short in the market. Generally, you are only short or long for one trade at a time (it is possible to be both long and short simultaneously, across different trades as a way of mitigating risk - however, this is an advanced trading technique). Because the cryptocurrency market can move extremely quickly, it is possible to be long in the morning and short in the afternoon within the same cryptocurrency.

There are two more market perspectives that are often talked about. If you expect prices to rise over the next few years, you are bullish on the market. If you expect prices to decline over the next few years, then you are bearish on the market. This is a very bullish book on cryptocurrency, even though it is a good idea to trade short on specific trades, at one time or another. When trading short you are merely taking advantage of the volatility to build your long-term investment capital with additional profits. We can do this by increasing the capital we have in the market through profiting on short trades and reinvesting this capital into our long-term investment portfolio over time in order to generate compounded profits and compounded results.

How To Grow Your Account Size For Free

There are two ways to increase any trading account. You can either fund the account with more of your own money or you can trade the account to take more capital from the market. Ideally, it is good to do both.

[T] In order to be as profitable as possible, you need an appropriate account size relative to your net worth. Only you can determine what level you feel comfortable to invest in any opportunity at any one time. If you are unsure as to how much capital you should be investing, use the free investment budget tool on the cryptoprof website (called 'Budget' on the 'Tools' menu).

Trading is as much of a psychological process as it is a technical skill. The technical tools I refer to in this chapter are only useful if they are used in the right way from a psychological basis. Panicking or using the tools without the correct psychological perspective will result in reduced profits. The psychology of trading is a skill set that is outside the scope of this book, but you can find additional resources on the website under the 'Psychology' tab on the 'Resources' menu.

Elliot Wave Theory

All markets are driven by the psychology of its participants. Every buyer and seller within a market is a person deciding to sell, maintain or buy more at a certain price. These movements can be interpreted by a system of analysis called Elliot Wave theory.

The theory allows an analyst to determine the most likely movement in the market using impulsive and corrective waves. There are a total of five waves in any movement where waves 1, 3 and 5 are impulsive and dramatic and waves 2 and 4 are corrective and go against the overall trend of the pattern.

For example, at the top left on the next page is a bullish five wave pattern which, overall, is a long trade, with small corrective shorts.

There is also a bearish wave pattern, which is the opposite of the bullish pattern (top right on the next page).

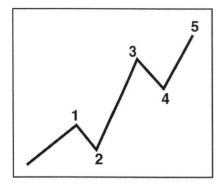
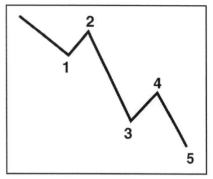

Each of these waves is itself made up of five waves in each of the movements. For example, the diagram below has waves 1, 3 and 5 on a larger scale showing the wave pattern inside each of the larger bullish movements.

This results in multiple levels of waves, all on different time scales, which can help you to determine where the price is likely to move over the next hour, day, week, year or even decade. It's possible to be bearish or bullish on one timeframe but the opposite perspective on another timeframe.

Generally, your long-term perspective on any market should be informed by an awareness of where you are in the larger market cycle. Up until recently, the larger market cycle for cryptocurrencies was bearish. However, recent bullish movement has led some

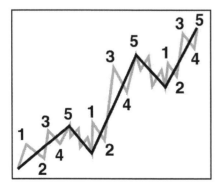

analysts to question whether we are transitioning into a long-term bullish market cycle. If this is the case, then you could not have chosen a better time to read this book. Whatever the case, you have a limited amount of time to make sure you can capture as many of these waves as possible to assist you in extracting the maximum amount of profit.

Support and Resistance

Looking at waves to construct your analysis is all well and good, but how can you determine when to enter and exit the market?

Within any market there are levels where the majority of buying and selling happens. These are called liquidity zones. It is at these liquidity zones where the price tends to pause before continuing or reversing its direction, based on the five-wave pattern we have just seen.

Below is a chart of bitcoin showing the liquidity zones on a one-hour chart at the end of May 2019. You can see that the ideal entry or exit prices are 7800, 7100 or 6300 euros. It is important to note that these prices are not exact but represent a window of around 200 euros

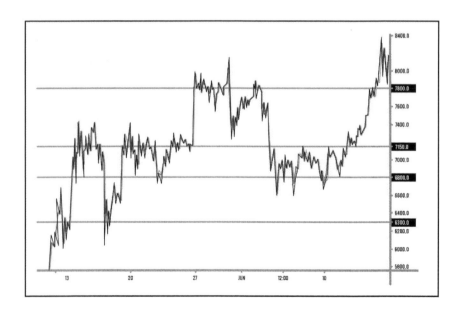

either side of the focus price. This price window represents a high probabilistic trade point for buying or selling rather than exact entry or exit points.

If the price reaches one of these liquidity zones and pauses within the liquidity window, then the price is more likely to reverse in direction. Seeing this resistance to further price movement, diligent traders will take a profit on at least one position, even at the risk of the position becoming more profitable after exiting the market. A banked profit means you have more flexibility on future trades rather than risk the trade becoming unprofitable if held and the price reversing back to unprofitability.

In an ideal situation, you should use multiple positions to ensure you take at least some profit, while retaining positions in the market to capture additional profit if the price continues in the same direction. The liquidity zones merely indicate that a change of direction is more likely than at any other price. If you are diligent with this strategy, you can take some profit while also still being exposed to the market. This policy can be captured in one simple rule: never sell all-out and never buy all-in.

If at any point you only have one position in the market, ask yourself whether you should have more exposure in order to have more flexibility. The more flexible you can be, the less likely you are to be caught off-guard if the market does something unexpected.

If you are not trading according to explicit positions, then consider selling 10% of your portfolio out at each liquidity zone and re-entering at the closest liquidity zone underneath the price where you sold out. This is an advanced trading strategy and you may benefit from additional training before utilising it. For more information please visit the 'Trading' tab under 'Resources' on the website.

Trading Versus Buy and Hold

Now you have seen some of the tools that you can use to trade cryptocurrencies, you may be wondering why you would go to all this effort to trade them? You could just buy and hold and not have to worry about analysis or getting in and out of the market in line with any single short-term trade perspective.

Buying and holding is what most investors who own cryptocurrency prefer to do, as trading takes a lot of skill and effort. They buy low and (try to) sell high, but on varying timescales depending on their strategy. They do not usually sell at the best price but tend to leave it too late and therefore experience reduced returns when compared with traders. With hindsight, anyone could say that everyone should have sold their bitcoin at $20,000, but the vast majority didn't.

Most investors become disillusioned with the market when their profitable positions turn negative (or even become a little less profitable). They sell out at a substantial loss when they should have been buying more. These individuals are trading with emotion as their central strategy, which is a recipe for poor returns and a frustrating, miserable investment experience. Trading using the methodology outlined in this book, and using the resources on the cryptoprof website, will make you more likely to enjoy good results. Every trade is executed according to the same method and there is no need for emotion to influence your trading decisions (though you will still feel strong emotions, and that's okay).

Trading cryptocurrencies has numerous advantages over buying and holding:

- It ensures you do take a profit (even if it is small) from the market.

- It allows you to benefit from both buying pressure (buying long) and selling pressure (selling short).

- You can trade on leverage (or extract out of positions) in order to increase your position size, without having to use additional capital.

- You can use tools such as trailing stops, stop-losses and automatic-take profits that are not available to people who just buy and hold.

There are also several negatives regarding trading, which you must mitigate or manage:

- If you sell out of a position automatically and the price continues to move profitably, then you do not get any additional benefit on that position.

- If you use leverage and your analysis is not correct, then you stand to take a larger loss than if you merely bought and held and 'weathered the storm' with dollar-cost-averaging.

- Trading is an intensive exercise that requires diligence, high-quality analysis, clear and critical thinking and strategies for risk management in addition to dealing with your emotions.

- When trading, there can be a disproportionately heavy focus on getting in and out of the market, so much so, that the long-term growth of positions is occasionally truncated for a comfortable profit.

There are ways to minimise the negatives of trading and maximise the positives:

- Always have multiple positions in the market. The more positions you have, the more flexible you can be when deciding to take profit or let the profit run.

- Use leverage sparingly and only when the technical analysis indicates a very strong trade.

- Set long-term and short-term positions in the market by building a portfolio. The long-term positions exist to ensure profitability from huge market movements while the short-term positions exist to benefit from volatility.

- Use tools such as trailing stops and stop-losses to ensure that the risk is appropriate for the return that you hope to generate. These tools can be used alongside long-term positions that you aim only to sell at the top of the market (when the time comes).

- Use advanced trading techniques such as opening a long and short position at the same price and taking a profit at different times.

By trading cryptocurrencies, you can take additional capital out of the market to reinforce your investment and yield additional profits on a long-term basis with compounding. You cannot do this through buying and holding where the only way to grow your investment is to put more of your own money into the market as the price fluctuates.

For example, below I have included a set of my own trade recommendations for bitcoin which would have yielded a 55% return over fifty-five days, if all trades had been implemented. Please bear in mind that this is not an exercise in hindsight trading - some of my clients were involved in every single trade. If they had been merely buying and holding, then their return would have been 0% over that fifty-five-day period rather than the 55% return they were able to generate from buying and selling based on the analysis at certain liquidity zones.

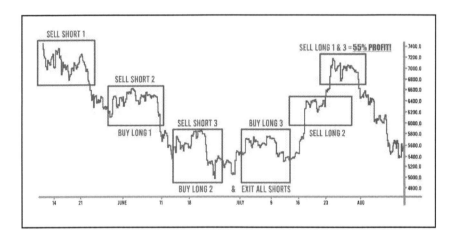

You And Your Investment

If you have read this far you have processed a lot of information about why investing in cryptocurrencies is likely to result in substantial profits over the next ten to twenty years.

You may now be wondering where to go next in order to start your investment journey. You have several options, all of which you can find under the 'Advanced' menu on the cryptoprof website.

1. You can sign up for the Introductory Investor program on the cryptoprof website. Here you will unlock free step-by-step guides and resources for building your own cryptocurrency investment portfolio. Select the 'Investor' tab to get started.

2. You can join the Total Trader program that will expand your trading knowledge and skills via online videos, tutorials, training events and a range of learning materials and tests to ensure you are expanding your knowledge. Select the 'Trader' tab to find out more.

3. If you would like to work directly with me to help you build and trade your portfolio, either on a one-to-one basis or with private group training, select the 'Personal' tab, add your information and I will contact you.

Final Thoughts

To bring this book to a close, I'll simply say that I hope you are now taking cryptocurrency investing a lot more seriously than before you read this book.

I have done my best to present my reasons for wanting to invest in cryptocurrencies in the early part of the 21st century. I hope that you agree with them. If you don't, maybe you should ask yourself if cryptocurrency investing is something you want to do? As you have seen, there are plenty of other investment options and opportunities, but none I feel are as exciting, potentially profitable and disruptive as cryptocurrencies.

I look forward to speaking with you and growing your profits over the months to come as we enter a new bull market for cryptocurrencies. If I were to offer a written prediction of the market movements by 2025, we should observe the prices to exceed the following for bitcoin, ether and ripple:

BTC: $100,000+

ETH: $3500+

XRP: $25+

Are you prepared to make the most of this? Start today!

About The Author

Peter Bryant is a senior broker and trader at an international private client asset management company.

He holds an MSc in Psychology from Goldsmiths, University of London and a music degree from the University of Surrey where he studied percussion and composition.

He is also a qualified psychotherapist registered with the United Kingdom Council of Psychotherapy (UKCP) as a hypno-psychotherapist.

He lives in Winchester with his wife Freya.

Acknowledgements

I would like to personally thank everyone who has been involved in this project. Without your support, this book would not have been written.

I would like to thank some of my clients for reading early drafts: Sarah Chadbourne, Barry Hanley, Richard Thompson, Trevor Loveland, David Nias, Tom Nash, Nick Light, and Naomi Light. I would also like to thank Sam Griffiths, Colin Harding and other attendees of First Friday in Winchester for their support with this project.

I would like to thank my wife, Freya, to whom this book is dedicated, as well as my parents, Elaine and Martin, who have encouraged and supported me from day one and continue to do so.

Thanks also must go to Neel Saund and Tim Hudson for giving advice to keep me motivated throughout, Levi Whale for always listening and having something nice to say and Adam Brice for kicking everything off for me.

Thank you to Laylah Garner for providing the excellent graphics and assisting with the book cover design and to Daniel Colbert for my headshot photograph. I would also like to thank Steve Baker for his assistance in producing the Crypto Profit eBook.

Finally, I would like to thank Ian Rowland. I have known Ian for almost a decade, and he continues to be one of the most enlightening, charming and interesting people I know. He is an experienced professional writer, among other things, and helped me to write and publish this book in a very short time. If you have a book inside you, Ian will help you to get it written, published and on sale. I suggest you check out his website (www.ianrowland.com).

Please Review This Book

If you have enjoyed reading Crypto Profit, I would really appreciate a short review on Amazon to help others decide to read this book. As a self-published author, word of mouth is extremely important for building an audience. High-quality reviews provide the conviction for someone who is entirely new to my work (or to cryptocurrencies in general) to read Crypto Profit and potentially make (or save) money. Thanks!

If you would like to get in touch with me directly, feel free to reach out to extras@thecryptoprof.com.

Printed in Great Britain
by Amazon